Site management (IYCB 2) Workbook

SITE MANAGEMENT

(IYCB 2) WORKBOOK

Claes-Axel Andersson
Derek Miles
Richard Neale
John Ward

International Labour Office   Geneva

Andersson, C. A., Miles, D., Neale, R. and Ward, J.
Site management (Improve Your Construction Business 2) Workbook
Geneva, International Labour Office, 1996
/Management development/, /Guide/, /Management/, /Construction/, /Small scale industry/, /Construction industry/. 12.04.1
ISBN 92-2-108754-9
ISBN for complete set of two volumes: 92-2-109315-8
ISSN 1020-0584

ILO Cataloguing in Publication Data

PREFACE

The *Improve your business (IYB)* approach to small enterprise development has proved its worth in many different countries, and has demonstrated the need for publications which are written simply and clearly but which can still communicate the basic management knowledge required by entrepreneurs if they are to run small businesses successfully.

Although all small businesses face some common problems and certain management principles are universal, experience has shown that a sector-specific development of the IYB approach would be widely welcomed.

This demand was particularly strong from enterprises in the construction sector, since small contractors have to cope with the special managerial problems that arise from bidding for and carrying out varied and dispersed projects. They are also faced with highly cyclical demand.

The ILO has responded by developing this Improve Your Construction Business (IYCB) series to suit the specific needs of small building and public works contractors. The IYCB series of three handbooks and three workbooks is available either separately or as a set, and comprises:

Pricing and bidding (IYCB 1): Handbook and Workbook

Site management (IYCB 2): Handbook and Workbook

Business management (IYCB 3): Handbook and Workbook.

They have been designed for self-study, but there is also an IYCB trainer's guide to assist trainers in preparing for and running seminars and workshops. As demand emerges, further handbooks and workbooks will be added to suit the specialist needs of, for example, road contractors and materials manufacturers.

The first handbook and workbook deal with pricing and bidding to obtain new projects. Too many contractors produce "guesstimates" not estimates – of project costs, so they either bid too high and lose the contract or – often even worse – get the work at a price which is below cost. The first handbook takes the reader step-by-step through the preparation of the bid for a small building contract, and also contains a contract glossary, while the workbook tests the reader's estimating skills and helps to identify the strengths and weaknesses of their businesses.

The second handbook and workbook start where the first set finishes – a potentially profitable contract has been won. The first part of these books, "planning for profit", helps the reader to prepare a realistic plan to carry out the work, while the second part, "making it happen", deals with the principles and practice of site supervision.

The third handbook and workbook cover business management. A contracting firm is not just a collection of individual contracts; it is also a business enterprise. These books focus on financial control and office administration, areas frequently neglected by contractors who are generally more interested in the technical aspects of building work.

The way the IYCB system works is that the *handbook* provides ideas and information and the *workbook* gives the reader a chance to look at his or her business in a disciplined way, and decide on action plans to make it more competitive and successful. Together, the IYCB series should enable you, as the owner or manager of a small construction enterprise, to improve *your* construction business. As joint authors, with between us about a hundred years' experience of working with small contractors around the world, we understand the risky and demanding environment in which you work and hope that the IYCB series will help you and your firm to survive and prosper.

This book was prepared and edited under the auspices of the ILO's Construction Management Programme, which was initiated within the Entrepreneurship and Management Development Branch of the Enterprise and Cooperative Development Department, and is now based in the Policies and Programmes for Development Branch of the Employment and Development Department.

Claes-Axel Andersson

Derek Miles

Richard Neale

John Ward

THE AUTHORS

Claes-Axel Andersson manages the Improve Your Construction Business project within the ILO Construction Management Programme, which is based in its Policies and Programmes for Development Branch. He is a professionally qualified civil engineer with extensive experience in project management and building design.

Derek Miles is Director of Overseas Activities in the Department of Civil Engineering at the Longhborough University of Technology, United Kingdom. He is a Fellow of the Institution of Civil Engineers and the Institute of Management and has more than 20 years' experience in the development of national construction industries. He directed the ILO Construction Management Programme during the period 1986-94.

Richard Neale is Senior Lecturer in the Department of Civil Engineering at the Loughborough University of Technology, United Kingdom. He is a professionally qualified civil engineer and builder, and is a consultant to the ILO and other international organizations in construction training and development.

John Ward is an independent consultant specializing in training for construction enterprises, and was previously chief technical adviser to the first Improve Your Construction Business project. He started his career as site agent and engineer with major construction companies, then ran his own small contracting business before specializing in the training of owners and managers of small construction enterprises.

ACKNOWLEDGEMENTS

The *Improve Your Business (IYB)* approach to small enterprise development was conceived by the Swedish Employers' Confederation, and has since been developed internationally by the ILO with financial assistance from the Swedish International Development Authority (SIDA) and other donors.

The Government of the Netherlands agreed to finance the first "Improve Your Construction Business" (IYCB) project, based at the Management Development and Productivity Institute (MDPI) in Accra.

Ghana proved a good choice. As a result of recent changes there is a more favourable climate for private sector initiatives, and Ghanaians have a well-deserved reputation for entrepreneurial drive. The Civil Engineering and Building Contractors Association of Ghana (CEBCAG) appreciated the opportunity that the project offered for its members to improve their management skills, and worked closely with the MDPI team and the ILO Chief Technical Adviser to ensure that the training programme met the most urgent needs of its members

This initial IYCB project provided an opportunity to develop and test a series of *Improve Your Construction Business* handbooks and workbooks and we wish to specifically acknowledge the dedication and enthusiasm of the MDPI/CEBCAG training teams or "cohorts".[1] The project package contained a certain amount of material that was specific to operating conditions in Ghana, but this published edition has been carefully edited to meet general needs of owners and managers of small-scale construction enterprises for basic advice on ways to improve business performance.

[1] Yahaya Abu, Michael Adjei, Margaret Agyemang, Kofitse Ahadzi, Henry Amoh-Mensa, Ernest Asare, John Asiedu, Franklin Badu, Fidelis Baku, Siegward Bakudie, Joseph Dick, Hamidu Haruna, Mathias Kudafa, D. Nsowah, Eric Ofori, Yaw Owusu-Kumih, S. Sakyi, Harry Seglah.

CONTENTS

Figures

HOW TO USE THIS WORKBOOK

This workbook is written for *you* – the owner or manager of a small construction business. Together the three basic IYCB handbooks provide advice on most aspects of running such a business, and the three complementary workbooks give you the chance to test your management skills and assess the performance of your business in a disciplined way, developing your own action plans.

Improve Your Construction Business is material for you to work with. It is available in a series of modules which take you step-by-step through the different stages of running a small contracting business. They are best read together. We suggest you first read the chapter in the handbook, and then work through the examples in the corresponding chapter of the workbook.

The handbook

The handbook contains a worked example of a simple building project, showing how to plan a typical project using bar charts, labour schedules, materials schedules, etc. It is both a basic text-book and a reference book, showing how you can plan your projects using a step-by-step approach. The chapters are set out in the same order as the chapters in the workbook, so that you can easily go from workbook to handbook or from handbook to workbook.

This workbook

This workbook enables you to test your planning skills by means of exercises in management practice. It will also make you think hard about how you can make your company more profitable by improving productivity on your sites.

In each chapter of this Workbook there is a list of simple questions to which you answer "yes" or "no". Your answers will tell you about the strengths and weaknesses of your business.

If you find that you need to improve your management skills in certain areas after going through the workbook, you can turn back to the appropriate section in the handbook and make sure you understand all the items and techniques introduced there.

Where to start

We recommend that you start by reading quickly through the whole of the handbook. Then you can go back over it more slowly, concentrating on the chapters which deal with those parts of management which you think are weakest in your business.

As soon as you feel comfortable with the ideas in a particular chapter, you can try out your skills in the workbook. Together this handbook and workbook, and the others in the IYCB series, should become your "business friends".

Note: Since this book is intended for use in many different countries, we have used the term "NU" in the examples to represent an imaginary National Unit of currency and NS to stand for imaginary National Standards.

PART A
PLANNING FOR PROFIT

CHOICE OF TECHNOLOGY   I

Quick reference

Ways of getting things done

This book is about getting things done on a construction site. Choice of technology means choosing how to carry out a particular project. Sometimes the choice is made by the consultant, but there are usually opportunities for the intelligent and experienced contractor to make decisions. It is particularly important to make correct decisions about the people to employ and the equipment to use, as these can result in better productivity and lower costs.

REMEMBER

❑ If you can't manage people and you call yourself a contractor, you are probably in the wrong business.

❑ Making the right choice of technology will help you to carry out your projects more quickly and at lower cost.

❑ Adaptability is a key construction skill.

❑ Concentrate on owning good basic equipment.

❑ Beware of losing business to competitors who have picked up new ideas and know more about the changing needs of clients.

Part 1 - Questions

		Yes	No
1.	Do you always think carefully about different ways of carrying out a project before choosing the best solution?.	☐	☐
2.	Do you try to learn new skills and new techniques?	☐	☐
3.	Do you use local materials whenever possible?. . .	☐	☐
4.	Do you have a reputation as a good employer? . .	☐	☐
5.	Do you own a concrete mixer?	☐	☐
6.	Do you own a pick-up truck?.	☐	☐
7.	Do you own steel scaffolding?	☐	☐
8.	Do you own steel formwork?.	☐	☐
9.	Do you only buy other equipment when you are reasonably sure you will make good use of it?. . . .	☐	☐
10.	Do you keep all your tools and equipment in good repair?.	☐	☐

Part 2 - Business practice

This section consists of an exercise to test your understanding of how to choose suitable technology.

EXERCISE 1   HOW TO DO IT

The following table lists a series of typical construction jobs. Go through the jobs one by one, and put a tick in the column to show whether you would use mostly labour or mostly equipment (and, if you choose equipment, which equipment you would use).

Job	Mostly labour	Mostly equipment (state type)
1. Site clearance – removal of light undergrowth		
2. Strip topsoil		
3. Excavate strip foundations		
4. Bulk fill to road base		
5. Rural feeder road construction		
6. Mix concrete for house floors		
7. Place concrete for house floors		
8. Place mass concrete fill		
9. Place timber roof trusses to houses		
10. Place steel roof trusses to factory workshops		
11. Build brick walls		
12. Build concrete block walls		
13. Place precast concrete wall panels		
14. Excavate trenches 1.5 - 2.0 metres deep		
15. Bed, lay and haunch sewer pipes		

Now check your answers

Our answers are at the end of this workbook. We suggest you check your answers against them before deciding on your action programme. If there is any disagreement, re-read Chapter 1 of the handbook to make sure you fully understand it.

Part 3 - Action programme

How to construct your action programme

Parts 1 and 2 should have helped you to recognize your strengths and weaknesses as the owner or manager of a construction enterprise. The general questions in Part 1 are a good guide to the strengths of your business and also to the areas where there is most room for improvement. So look back and count the number of times you answered "yes" or "no".

How many times did you answer "yes"? The more "yes" answers, the more likely it is that your business will do well.

Now look again at those questions where you answered "no". These may be problem or opportunity areas for your business. Choose the one which is most important at the present time. This is the sensible way to improve your business. Take the most urgent problem first. Don't try to solve everything at once.

Now write the problem or opportunity into the following action programme, as we have done with the example. Then write in <u>What must be done</u>, <u>By whom</u> and <u>By when</u> in order to make sure things improve.

Finally, go back to your business and carry out the action programme.

Problem	What must be done	By whom?	By when?
Imported materials are too costly	Try to locate locally-produced alternatives	Self and foreman	1 July

ALLOWABLES 2

Quick reference

❏ The direct project costs are used to calculate the allowables.

❏ If the actual costs are lower than the allowables, you will make a profit.

❏ If the actual costs are higher than the allowables, you will make a loss.

REMEMBER

❏ Planning means looking forward, making preparations and deciding on the best course of action.

❏ Cost allowables are those costs which are allowed to cover labour, plant and transport used on the job.

❏ Time allowables are the number of work-hours that can be allowed to complete one unit of any item.

❏ Cost allowables can be used for cost control on the site.

❏ Time allowables can be used for planning the most cost-effective period for completing a job.

Part 1 - Questions

		Yes	No
1.	Do you know how to calculate labour cost allowables?	☐	☐
2.	Do you know how to calculate plant cost allowables?	☐	☐
3.	Do you know how to calculate transport cost allowables?	☐	☐
4.	Do you know how to calculate labour time allowables?	☐	☐
5.	Do you know how to calculate plant time allowables?	☐	☐
6.	Do you know how to calculate transport time allowables?	☐	☐
7.	Do you know how to prepare an allowables chart?	☐	☐
8.	Do you know how to calculate the most cost-effective time period?	☐	☐
9.	Do you keep records of allowables calculations from previous jobs?	☐	☐
10.	Do you check whether cost and time allowables are gradually reducing as the efficiency of your firm improves?	☐	☐

Part 2 - Business practice

Exercise 1   COMPLETE THE ALLOWABLES

Pages 12 to 14 show a direct project costs chart and a chart indicating the estimated time needed to complete each activity for one of the buildings in our example in the appendix to the Handbook. From the charts on pp. 12-14 work out the labour, plant and transport cost allowables and the labour time allowables for the following items:

Nos. 2, 3, 5, 6, 7, 8, 10, 11, 12, 13, 17 and 18.

ALLOWABLES CHART

Item no.	Description	Unit	Cost allowables			Time allowables		
			Labour	Plant	Transport	Labour	Plant	Transport

DIRECT PROJECT COSTS CHART FOR ONE BUILDING

Item no.	Description	Unit	Quantity	Labour	Plant	Material	Transport	Total
	List of quantities taken off drawings			Direct project costs (NU)				
1.	Excavate foundations	m³	25	125				125
2.	Steel to foundations 12 mm 8 mm	m	300 72	78		207	2	287
3.	Formwork to foundations	m²	18	52		39	3	94
4.	Concrete to foundations	m³	4.0	28	8	103	20	159
5.	Steel to columns 12 mm 8 mm	m	231 76	104		165	2	271
6.	Formwork to columns	m²	49	104		82	5	191
7.	Pour concrete to columns	m³	3.7	112	32	95	18	257
8.	Concrete block walls up to floor	m²	32	93		399	30	522
9.	Return fill and ram excavated material around foundations	m³	17	39				39
10.	Hardcore fill	m³	17	84	24	124	10	242
11.	Mesh to floor	m²	51	52		108	1	161
12.	Concrete to floor	m³	6.8	168	48	175	31	422
13.	Concrete block walls above floor	m²	34	93		427	33	553
14.	Soffit forms to ring beam over openings	m²	3	26		5	1	32
15.	Soffit forms over infill panels	m²	2.2	26		4	1	31
						Subtotal (items 1-15)		3 386

\multicolumn{5}{l}{List of quantities taken off drawings}					Direct project costs (NU)				
Item no.	Description	Unit	Quantity	Labour	Plant	Material	Transport	Total
16.	Sideforms to ring beam	m²	18	78		30	2	110
17.	Supply and fix steel 12 mm to ring beam 8 mm	m	144 54	78		105	2	185
18.	Pour concrete to ring beam	m³	2.6	112	32	67	12	223
19.	Fabricate roof trusses	No.	11	104		244	7	355
20.	Fix roof trusses	No.	11	52		17	1	70
21.	Roof tile battens	m	212	13		47	2	62
22.	Tile roof (including ridge)	m²	81	69		961	17	1047
23.	Timber to gable end	m²	6	26		44	2	72
24.	Form eaves horizontal and gable ends	m	36	26		49	1	76
25.	Supply and fix ceiling boards	m²	42	18		185	5	208
26.	Prefabricated window panels	No.	4	36		300		336
27.	Prefabricated door panels	No.	1	18		100		118
28.	Terrazzo floor	m²	44	36	10	100	1	147
29.	Plaster walls and columns and ringbeam	m²	48	52		25	6	83
30.	Paint walls and ceilings	m²	90	42		135	5	182
						Final total (items 1-30)		6 660

ESTIMATED TIME NEEDED TO COMPLETE ITEM

Item no.	Description	Estimated time needed to complete activity (days)	Labourers needed	
			skilled	general
1.	Excavate foundations	5.0		5
2.	Steel reinforcement to foundations	3.0	2	2
3.	Formwork to foundations	2.0	2	2
4.	Concrete to foundations	0.5	2	8
5.	Steel reinforcement to columns	4.0	2	2
6.	Formwork to columns	4.0	2	2
7.	Concrete to columns	2.0	2	8
8.	Concrete block walls up to floor	3.0	2	3
9.	Return fill and ram excavated material around foundations	3.0	1	1
10.	Hardcore fill	3.0	1	4
11.	Mesh to floor	2.0	2	2
12.	Concrete to floor	3.0	2	8
13.	Concrete block walls above floor	3.0	2	3
14.	Soffit forms to ring beam, openings	2.0	1	1
15.	Soffit forms to ring beam, infill panels	2.0	1	1
16.	Sideforms to ring beam	3.0	2	2
17.	Steel to ring beam	3.0	2	2
18.	Concrete to ring beam	2.0	2	8
19.	Fabricate roof trusses	4.0	2	2
20.	Fix roof trusses	2.0	2	2
21.	Roof tile battens	1.0	1	1
22.	Tile roof	3.0	1	3
23.	Timber to gable ends	2.0	1	1
24.	Form eaves	2.0	1	1
25.	Supply and fix ceiling boards	1.0	1	2
26.	Fix prefabricated window panels	2.0	1	2
27.	Fix prefabricated door panels	1.0	1	2
28.	Terrazzo floor	2.0	1	2
29.	Bagwash walls and columns	4.0	1	1
30.	Paint	2.0	2	1

A blockmaker has won a contract to supply 100,000 blocks to a site 10 km from the yard. One thousand blocks can be made per day. As you can see, the costs have been studied carefully and the following information is available.

Daily costs:

Ten labourers @ two NU each	20 NU
Mixer, including fuel	20 NU
Cement and aggregates	60 NU

The blockmaker also has a truck which can transport 1,000 blocks a day to the site:
Truck, including driver and fuel,
depreciation, maintenance, insurance,
licences and overheads   40 NU

The blockmaker wishes to make a 25 per cent profit on the sale of the blocks, and also wants to know the cost allowables for making 100 blocks.

This question has two parts:

A. What are the labour, plant and transport cost allowables per 100 blocks?

B. What will be the final cost to the client per 100 blocks delivered to site (excluding indirect costs)?

Now check your answers

Our answers are at the end of this workbook. We suggest you check your answers against them before deciding on your action programme. If there is any disagreement, re-read Chapter 2 of the handbook to make sure you fully understand it.

Part 3 - Action programme

How to construct your action programme

Parts 1 and 2 should have helped you to recognize your strengths and weaknesses as the owner or manager of a construction enterprise. The general questions in Part 1 are a good guide to the strengths of your business and also to the areas where there is most room for improvement. So look back and count the number of times you answered "yes" or "no".

How many times did you answer "yes"? The more "yes" answers, the more likely it is that your business will do well. Now look again at those questions where you answered "no". These may be problem or opportunity areas for your business. Choose the one which is most important at the present time. This is the sensible way to improve your business. Take the most urgent problem first. Don't try to solve everything at once.

Now write the problem or opportunity into the following action programme, as we have done with the example. Then write in <u>What must be done</u>, <u>By whom</u> and <u>By when</u> in order to make sure things improve.

Finally, go back to your business and carry out the action programme.

Problem	What must be done	By whom?	By when?
I cannot plan my workload due to lack of information	Keep records of allowables calculations from previous jobs	Self	Start now

BAR CHARTS   3

Quick reference

❑ You should always try and prepare a realistic time schedule for the job.

❑ This time schedule should be prepared at a very early stage in the job.

❑ The time schedule is called a "bar chart", because each activity is shown as a bar with specified starting and finishing dates.

REMEMBER

❑ The bar chart is a picture of how the work is going to be carried out.

❑ The bar chart shows how the various operations fit together.

❑ There are six steps to preparing a bar chart:

1. Plan.

2. List jobs.

3. Calculate quantities.

4. Calculate time.

5. Draw the bar chart.

6. Check.

Part 1 - Questions

Yes No

1. Do you always prepare a bar chart when bidding
   for a job? . . . . ☐ ☐

2. Do you review and update the chart when the job
   is awarded? . . . . ☐ ☐

3. Do you make sure that your foremen understand
   bar charts? . . . . ☐ ☐

4. Do you make sure that the bar chart is displayed
   in the site office? . . . . ☐ ☐

5. Do you make sure that the bar chart is kept up to
   date with corrections as the job goes along? . . . . . ☐ ☐

6. Do you compare performance on different jobs
   by comparing updated bar charts? . . . . ☐ ☐

7. Do you know which operations can be done at
   the same time? . . . . ☐ ☐

8. Do you know which operations must be finished
   before others can start? . . . . ☐ ☐

9. Do you know which operations can overlap
   with others? . . . . ☐ ☐

10. Do you always know if you are making the best
    use of your resources? . . . . ☐ ☐

Part 2 - Business practice

Exercise 1   CONCRETE FLOOR SLAB

Prepare a bar chart for a subcontract to build a concrete floor
slab from the following information. Your contract is the first on
site so some preparatory work is included:

Activity 1: Build access road   3 weeks
Activity 2: Fence site   2 weeks
Activity 3: Strip topsoil   1 week
Activity 4: Spread hardcore over site   2 weeks
Activity 5: Seal hardcore with lean mix concrete   2 weeks
Activity 6: Fix steel mesh for floor slab   4 weeks
Activity 7: Pour concrete to floor slab and cure   7 weeks
Activity 8: Clear site   1 week

NOW CHECK YOUR ANSWERS

Our answers are at the end of this workbook. We suggest you check your answers against them before deciding on your action programme. If there is any disagreement, re-read Chapter 3 of the handbook to make sure you fully understand it.

BAR CHART - CONCRETE FLOOR SLABS

Item	Week number

Part 3 - Action programme

How to construct your action programme

Parts 1 and 2 should have helped you to recognize your strengths and weaknesses as the owner or manager of a construction enterprise. The general questions in Part 1 are a good guide to the strengths of your business and also to the areas where there is most room for improvement. So look back and count the number of times you answered "yes" or "no".

How many times did you answer "yes"? The more "yes" answers, the more likely it is that your business will do well. Now look again at those questions where you answered "no". These may be problem or opportunity areas for your business. Choose the one which is most important at the present time. This is the sensible way to improve your business. Take the most urgent problem first. Don't try to solve everything at once.

Now write the problem or opportunity into the following action programme, as we have done with the example. Then write in <u>What must be done</u>, <u>By whom</u> and <u>By when</u> in order to make sure things improve.

Finally, go back to your business and carry out the action programme.

Problem	What must be done	By whom?	By when?
It is very difficult to keep to a time schedule and to know when my jobs are falling behind	Draw up a bar chart at the start of the job and keep it up to date	Self	At the start of each job

LABOUR SCHEDULES 4

Quick reference

❏ If you have difficulty in allocating labour productively, you should learn how to make labour schedules.

❏ Labour schedules are made from bar charts.

❏ If you make and follow labour schedules you should be able to utilize your workforce more efficiently.

❏ A more efficient workforce will produce more profit.

REMEMBER

❏ A labour schedule shows you the workforce you need and when it should be on site.

❏ A labour schedule with an even spread shows good utilization of labour.

❏ An uneven spread shows poor utilization and should be evened out.

❏ A change in the workforce could lead to a change in the programme and alterations to the bar chart.

Part 1 - Questions

	Yes	No
1. Do you know how to prepare a labour schedule?	☐	☐
2. Do you generally keep your workers steadily employed?	☐	☐
3. Do you make good use of your skilled workers? .	☐	☐
4. Do you make sure that workers are not suddenly switched from one job to another?	☐	☐
5. Do you make sure that you only employ capable workers?.	☐	☐
6. Do you compare the time the job takes to the cost of the labour used on it?.	☐	☐
7. Do you know how many workers are required for each job?	☐	☐
8. Do you have standby jobs available for workers who are temporarily surplus on other jobs?	☐	☐
9. Do you schedule workers in advance for essential but non-productive jobs such as tidying the site? .	☐	☐
10. Do you avoid having to hire casual labour as a panic measure by planning labour needs in advance? . . .	☐	☐

Part 2 - Business practice

Exercise 1   CAN YOU DELIVER?

You have a small workshop and you are planning to bid for a contract to supply 200 hardwood door frames and 1,000 hardwood window frames for a housing contract. The site is located half a day's drive from your workshop. The sawmill is one day's drive from the workshop and the timber will be collected by a truck that you will have to hire especially for this purpose. It takes about half a day for four labourers to load at the sawmill and another half day to unload at the workshop. Four separate journeys will be needed before all the rough timber reaches the workshop.

In the workshop you have two circular saws and two planers, but all the finishing jointing, moulding and fixing must be done by hand.

You must also hire a truck to deliver the finished frames. You will need five deliveries and it takes approximately half a day for four labourers to load the finished material at the workshop and one half day to unload at the site.

In the bidding documents it says that the finished material must be delivered to site within eight weeks or the manufacturer will have to pay substantial damages to the client for each week the completion is delayed.

Your task is to draw up a bar chart and labour schedules to determine whether you can deliver within eight weeks.

You have only four carpenters available but there is no shortage of general labourers who can be hired on a weekly basis.

On this bar chart, all the activities are listed:

BAR CHART, MANUFACTURING OF FRAMES

Item	Week number							
	01	02	03	04	05	06	07	08
1. Collect materials								
2. Cut to size								
3. Plane timber								
4. Moulding and jointing								
5. Fix frames								
6. Varnish								
7. Deliver to site								

The following number of workweeks (no. of workers × no. of weeks) are needed for the different items:

WORKWEEKS NEEDED

Item	Carpenters	General labourers
1. Collect materials		10
2. Cut to size	3	6
3. Plane timber	4	8
4. Moulding and jointing	12	6
5. Fix frames	10	5
6. Varnish	8	4
7. Deliver to site		8

SEMI-WEEKLY LABOUR SCHEDULE, CARPENTERS

Item	Week number							
	01	02	03	04	05	06	07	08
1. Collect materials								
2. Cut to size								
3. Plane timber								
4. Moulding and jointing								
5. Fix frames								
6. Varnish								
7. Deliver to site								
Totals								

SEMI-WEEKLY LABOUR SCHEDULE, GENERAL LABOURERS

Item	Week number							
	01	02	03	04	05	06	07	08
1. Collect materials								
2. Cut to size								
3. Plane timber								
4. Moulding and jointing								
5. Fix frames								
6. Varnish								
7. Deliver to site								
Totals								

Now check your answers

Our answers are at the end of this workbook. We suggest you check your answers against them before deciding on your action programme. If there is any disagreement, re-read Chapter 4 of the handbook to make sure you fully understand it.

Part 3 - Action programme

How to construct your action programme

Parts 1 and 2 should have helped you to recognize your strengths and weaknesses as the owner or manager of a construction enterprise. The general questions in Part 1 are a good guide to the strengths of your business and also to the areas where there is most room for improvement. So look back and count the number of times you answered "yes" or "no".

How many times did you answer "yes"? The more "yes" answers, the more likely it is that your business will do well. Now look again at those questions where you answered "no".

These may be problem or opportunity areas for your business. Choose the one which is most important at the present time. This is the sensible way to improve your business. Take the most urgent problem first. Don't try to solve everything at once.

Now write the problem or opportunity into the following action programme, as we have done with the example. Then write in <u>What must be done</u>, <u>By whom</u> and <u>By when</u> in order to make sure things improve.

Finally, go back to your business and carry out the action programme.

Problem	What must be done	By whom?	By when?
It is very difficult to keep regular employees working profitably	Always prepare labour schedules and plan the hiring of labour in advance	Self	Start now

PLANT
AND TRANSPORT SCHEDULES   5

Quick reference

❑ If you have difficulty in allocating plant and transport productively, you should learn how to make plant and transport
schedules.

❑ Plant and transport schedules are based mainly on information from the bar chart.

❑ If you make and follow plant and transport schedules you
should be able to use your items of plant and transport more
efficiently, no matter whether you hire them or own them.

❑ More efficient use of plant and transport will result in more
profit.

REMEMBER

❑ A plant and transport schedule shows you what is needed
and when it should be on site.

❑ The schedule can help you to decide what to hire and what
to buy.

❑ The effective use of a plant and transport schedule can lead
to significant cost savings.

Part 1 - Questions

		Yes	No
1.	Do you know how to prepare a plant and transport schedule?........................	☐	☐
2.	Do you generally keep your plant regularly in use?.	☐	☐
3.	Do you make sure that plant is regularly maintained?	☐	☐
4.	Do you make sure that concrete mixers are cleaned out after use?......................	☐	☐
5.	Do you make sure that shovels and other hand tools are cleaned after use?..............	☐	☐
6.	Do you compare the time the job takes to the output of the plant used on it?	☐	☐
7.	Do you know which items of plant to use on each operation?..........................	☐	☐
8.	Do you have standby jobs available so as to get full use out of your plant?...................	☐	☐
9.	Do you schedule plant in advance for essential but non-productive tasks such as tidying the site?.	☐	☐
10.	Do you make sure that you never have to hire in expensive plant as a panic measure?	☐	☐

Part 2 - Business practice

Exercise 1   PLANT AND TRANSPORT SCHEDULES

You have won a contract to construct a 50 m x 20 m gravel sur-
faced car park.

Specification:

1. Strip topsoil (approximately 0.10 m deep) and cart to stor-
    age area 1 km from site

2. Excavate remaining ground to a total depth of 0.25 m below
    ground level (dump 2 km away)

3. Fill to 0.10 m below ground level with crushed brick hard-
    core as supplied by client from demolished buildings 4 km
    from site. Hardcore to be compacted by roller

4. Fill to ground level with gravel from approved borrow pit to
    ground level. Gravel to be compacted by roller

5. Contractor will be responsible for providing plant to load
    hardcore and gravel from borrow pit 8 km from site

6. Contractor is expected to provide the client with a list of
    quantities, bar chart and a plant and transport schedule
    before work starts

Complete the list of quantities, make a bar chart and a plant
and transport schedule.

LIST OF QUANTITIES

Item	Description	Unit	Quantity
1	Strip topsoil and cart to storage area	m³	
2	Excavate ground and cart to dump	m³	
3	Load hardcore, spread, level and compact	m³	
4	Load gravel, spread, level and compact	m³	

29

Based on your previous experience you intend to use one front-end loader and two 6 m³ tipper trucks for items 1 and 2.

For items 3 and 4 you are planning to use one front-end loader, four 6 m³ tippers, one grader and one roller.

Item 1: It takes about one hour for the tipper truck to load, drive to the storage area, tip and return to the site.

Item 2: It takes two hours to load the truck, drive to the dump, tip and return to the site.

Item 3: It takes three hours to drive to the demolition site to get the hardcore, load the truck, drive back and tip. We need the grader for four days and the roller for five days.

Item 4: It takes four hours to load the gravel, travel to the site, tip and return. We need the grader for four days and the roller for five days.

As you can see from the bar chart and plant and transport schedule on the following pages, we intend to show duration of activities per full day.

Now check your answers

Our answers are at the end of this workbook. We suggest you check your answers against them before deciding on your action programme. If there is any disagreement, re-read Chapter 5 of the handbook to make sure you fully understand it.

BAR CHART

Item	Day number																													
	1	2	3	4	5	6	7	8	9	10	11	12	13	14	15	16	17	18	19	20	21	22	23	24	25	26	27	28	29	30
1. Strip topsoil and cart																														
2. Excavate ground and dump																														
3a. Load hardcore and tip																														
3b. Spread and level																														
3c. Compact																														
4a. Load gravel and tip																														
4b. Spread and level																														
4c. Compact																														

PLANT AND TRANSPORT SCHEDULE

Item	Day number																													
	1	2	3	4	5	6	7	8	9	10	11	12	13	14	15	16	17	18	19	20	21	22	23	24	25	26	27	28	29	30
1. Strip top-soil and cart																														
2. Excavate ground and dump																														
3a. Load hardcore and tip																														
3b. Spread and level																														
3c. Compact																														

4a. Load gravel and tip	4b. Spread and level	4c. Compact	Front-end loader	6 m^3 tipper trucks	Grader	Roller

Part 3 - Action programme

How to construct your action programme

Parts 1 and 2 should have helped you to recognize your strengths and weaknesses as the owner or manager of a construction enterprise. The general questions in Part 1 are a good guide to the strengths of your business and also to the areas where there is most room for improvement. So look back and count the number of times you answered "yes" or "no".

How many times did you answer "yes"? The more "yes" answers, the more likely it is that your business will do well. Now look again at those questions where you answered "no".

These may be problem or opportunity areas for your business. Choose the one which is most important at the present time. This is the sensible way to improve your business. Take the most urgent problem first. Don't try to solve everything at once.

Now write the problem or opportunity into the following action programme, as we have done with the example. Then write in <u>What must be done</u>, <u>By whom</u> and <u>By when</u> in order to make sure things improve.

Finally, go back to your business and carry out the action programme.

Problem	What must be done	By whom?	By when?
It is very difficult to keep my plant fully employed	Always prepare plant schedules and plan the hiring of plant in advance	Self	Start now

MATERIALS SCHEDULES 6

Quick reference

❑ If you experience problems with the delivery of materials by suppliers, you should learn to make materials schedules.

❑ If you find yourself ordering materials in a haphazard fashion at the last minute, and thus paying too much for them, you can benefit by using materials schedules.

❑ If you are losing money due to wastage of materials, you should make and use materials schedules.

REMEMBER

❑ Materials schedules are used for ordering materials.

❑ They are drawn up during the planning stage.

❑ With a materials schedule you can make sure that the materials are on site when they are needed.

Part 1 - Questions

	Yes	No

1. Do you know how to prepare
   a materials schedule?.......................... ☐ ☐

2. Do you review and update your materials
   schedule whenever a new drawing or instruction
   is received from the consultant?............... ☐ ☐

3. Do you make sure you order materials that exactly
   match those specified by the consultant?........ ☐ ☐

4. Do you make sure that quantities ordered match
   those required with a reasonable allowance
   for wastage?................................. ☐ ☐

5. Do you make sure that the supplier has exact
   delivery instructions (place and date)?.......... ☐ ☐

6. Do you compare quotations from alternative
   suppliers?.................................. ☐ ☐

7. Do you know all the paragraphs in the standard
   specifications?.............................. ☐ ☐

8. Do you make sure that your foreman has an
   up-to-date copy of the materials schedule
   to check deliveries?.......................... ☐ ☐

9. Do you make sure cement is kept dry until
   it is used?.................................. ☐ ☐

10. Do you make sure all materials are properly
    stacked and kept securely stored on site?........ ☐ ☐

Part 2 - Business practice

Exercise 1

COMPLETE THE MATERIALS SCHEDULE

In Chapter 6 in the handbook a materials schedule was filled in covering the first six orders for our exercise project on the buildings at Wardoboyo illustrated at the back of the handbook. Fill in the materials schedule for the rest of the items using the revised bar chart and the quantities that were taken off during the materials calculations.

The items are: 27. Ceiling boards; 28. Window panels; 29. Door panels; 30. Terrazzo; 32. Paint.

Assume that the time lags between ordering and delivery are as follows:

Door panels	2 weeks
Window panels	1 week
Ceiling boards	2 weeks
Paint	1 week
Terrazzo	1 week

Week 15 starts on 7 November, Week 20 starts on 12 December.

Delivery is planned for the beginning of the week even if the bar chart tells you the activity should start in the middle of the week.

MATERIALS SCHEDULE, EXERCISE 1

Information obtained from calculations of quantities				Date that materials are needed on site (from bar chart)	Time needed between order and delivery (information at planning stage)	Latest date that order must be placed	Details of supplier					
Item	Description	Unit	Quantity				Order no.	Name	Address	Phone	Contact	Remarks
27.	Ceiling boards						205	Best Company	Border Road 8	3249	Steve Neale	Allows 2 weeks credit
28.	Window panels						211	G Workshop Ltd.	Long Road 32	1145	Mr. Stone	Cash on delivery
29.	Door panels						212	Frame Works Ltd.	Panel Road 21	2988	Mr. Knob	Cash with order
30.	Terrazzo						220	Floor Special Ltd.	Fifth Street 112	8834	Dick	Cash on delivery
32.	Paint						250	Color Company	Drum Street	6487	Mr. Roller	Allows 3 weeks credit

USING THE MATERIALS SCHEDULE

You have won a subcontract to supply and fix all the carpentry /joinery items for a rural clinic. The site storage space is limited and you are not allowed to store your materials on site for longer than two weeks before they are due to be fixed. You have a long-standing arrangement with a joinery workshop which supplies and delivers materials at a very reasonable price. All the items to be supplied must be ordered eight weeks in advance. The main contractor's site agent gives you a bar chart and requests a materials schedule. At this stage the excavation of the foundations has just started.

This exercise requires that you:

A. Draw up a materials schedule and then answer two questions:

B. Can you keep to the main contractor's programme?

C. If it is difficult to keep pace with the main contractor, what are the major reasons for this?

The joinery workshop has quoted the following production schedule for the items required for the clinic:

10 door frames	1 week
40 window frames	3 weeks
35 roof trusses	4 weeks
40 bedsite units	4 weeks
10 doors	1 week
40 timber partition screens	2 weeks

The workshop does not have the capacity to work on more than one item at a time, i.e. the door frames have to be completed before the workshop can start on the window frames, and so on.

See the contractor's bar chart, on pp. 40-41.

Now check your answers

Our suggested answers are at the end of this workbook. We suggest you check your answers against them before deciding on your action programme. If there is any disagreement, re-read Chapter 6 of the handbook to make sure you fully understand it.

Item	Week number
	1 2 3 4 5 6 7 8 9 10 11 12 13 14 15 16 17 18 19 20 21 22 23 24 25 26 27 28 29 30 31 32 33 34 35 36 37 38 39 40
1. Strip topsoil	
2. Excavate foundations	
3. Build to floor level	
4. Fit door frames	
5. Build to sill level	
6. Fit window frames	
7. Build to ring beams	
8. Cast ringbeam/ cure	

9. Fit roof trusses

10. Complete roof

11. Fit ceilings

12. Plaster

13. Fit bedside units

14. Plumbing

15. Electrical installations

16. Fit doors

17. Finishings

18. Fit partition screens

19. Paint

MATERIALS SCHEDULE, EXERCISE 2

Information obtained from calculations of quantities				Date that materials are needed on site (from bar chart)	Time needed between order and delivery (information at planning stage)	Latest date that order must be placed	Details of supplier					Remarks
Item	Description	Unit	Quantity				Order no.	Name	Address	Phone	Contact	

Part 3 - Action programme

How to construct your action programme

Parts 1 and 2 should have helped you to recognize your strengths and weaknesses as the owner or manager of a construction enterprise. The general questions in Part 1 are a good guide to the strengths of your business and also to the areas where there is most room for improvement. So look back and count the number of times you answered "yes" or "no".

How many times did you answer "yes"? The more "yes" answers, the more likely it is that your business will do well. Now look again at those questions where you answered "no". These may be problem or opportunity areas for your business. Choose the one which is most important at the present time. This is the sensible way to improve your business. Take the most urgent problem first. Don't try to solve everything at once.

Now write the problem or opportunity into the following action programme, as we have done with the example. Then write in <u>What must be done</u>, <u>By whom</u> and <u>By when</u> in order to make sure things improve.

Finally, go back to your business and carry out the action programme.

Problem	What must be done	By whom?	By when?
Cement is going hard in the shed and cannot be used	Make sure that cement is always stored in a dry shed and that it is used in order of delivery so that it will not deteriorate	Self and Foreman	Now

CHECKING ON PROGRESS   7

Quick reference

The future can never be predicted accurately and as a contractor you know that this is especially true for construction projects. When you plan the project you know that not everything will happen the way you predict it.

There are many factors that can delay a project such as absenteeism, breakdowns, heavy rains and delayed payments, and these problems have to be dealt with when they happen.

When things go wrong, you do not want to be forced into taking decisions without thinking through the consequences. This means you should check on progress regularly, so that you have the earliest possible warning of something going wrong.

Your prepared bar chart is very important when something has happened that makes it impossible to follow the plans. Your chart then helps you to predict the impact a change will have on other activities of the project.

Follow-up and planning have to continue throughout the project.

We call this process "Checking on progress".

REMEMBER

❑ Progress made on the project should be regularly marked up on the bar chart.

❑ When things start to go wrong the project will probably start to fall behind schedule.

❑ Planning must be flexible.

❑ Work can be replanned to finish on time only if you are aware that the project is falling behind schedule.

Part 1 - Questions

		Yes	No
1.	Do you always keep your project bar charts up to date?	☐	☐
2.	Do you always keep labour schedules up to date?	☐	☐
3.	Do you always keep materials schedules up to date?	☐	☐
4.	Do you always keep plant and transport schedules up to date?	☐	☐
5.	Do you make sure that your foremen know how to use charts and schedules?	☐	☐
6.	Do you compare bar charts from various jobs? . .	☐	☐
7.	Do you take action immediately a project starts to fall behind schedule?	☐	☐
8.	Do you make sure that the planning of your bar chart is flexible enough to cope with sudden emergencies?	☐	☐
9.	Do you advise the consultant of any likely changes in project progress as soon as they become clear from updating your bar chart?	☐	☐
10.	Do you discuss with your foreman ways of bringing the job back on schedule if progress has fallen behind the targets on the bar chart?	☐	☐

Part 2 - Business practice

Exercise 1   MARKING UP THE BAR CHART

Using the bar charts supplied, mark up progress as follows, using the method shown in the example.

Section A. At the end of Week 4, concrete to foundations is one week behind schedule.

Section B. At the end of Week 8 concrete to columns is two weeks behind schedule, but the steel to the ring-beam has been prefabricated and the roof trusses have been made ready for fixing.

Section C. At the end of Week 11 the pouring of concrete to the columns is not finished, you have started to clear the site. The steel and shuttering to the ringbeam have been prefabricated and the roof trusses have been made.

Exercise 2   BACK ON SCHEDULE

The completed bar chart on pages 54 to 55 shows that the work is four weeks behind schedule at the end of Week 14. How can the project be brought back on schedule to finish at the end of Week 20? Use the chart supplied on pages 56 to 57.

Exercise 3   A FEEDER-ROAD CONTRACT

Section A. What does the completed bar chart on page 58 tell you?

Section B. Draw up a revised bar chart to get the feeder-road contract completed on schedule.

Section C. What changes will the contractor have to make in order to complete the whole contract on schedule?

BAR CHART - CONSTRUCTION PHASE

Section A

Item	Week number																			
	01	02	03	04	05	06	07	08	09	10	11	12	13	14	15	16	17	18	19	20
1. Excavate foundations		█																		
2. Fix steel foundations			█																	
3. Pour concrete to foundations				█																
4. Fix steel to columns					█															
5. Fix formwork to columns						█														
6. Pour concrete to columns							█													

7. Fix steel to ringbeam	8. Fix formwork to ringbeam	9. Pour concrete to ringbeam	10. Fabricate and fix roof trusses	11. Tile roof	12. Fit infill panels	13. Fix ceiling	14. Fit and glaze windows	15. Paint	16. Clear site

Section B

Item	Week number																			
	01	02	03	04	05	06	07	08	09	10	11	12	13	14	15	16	17	18	19	20
1. Excavate foundations	▮	▮																		
2. Fix steel foundations		▮	▮																	
3. Pour concrete to foundations			▮	▮																
4. Fix steel to columns				▮	▮															
5. Fix formwork to columns					▮	▮														
6. Pour concrete to columns						▮	▮													

50

7. Fix steel to ringbeam

8. Fix formwork to ringbeam

9. Pour concrete to ringbeam

10. Fabricate and fix roof trusses

11. Tile roof

12. Fit infill panels

13. Fix ceiling

14. Fit and glaze windows

15. Paint

16. Clear site

Section C

Item	Week number																			
	01	02	03	04	05	06	07	08	09	10	11	12	13	14	15	16	17	18	19	20
1. Excavate foundations	‖	‖																		
2. Fix steel foundations		‖	‖																	
3. Pour concrete to foundations			‖	‖																
4. Fix steel to columns				‖	‖															
5. Fix formwork to columns					‖	‖														
6. Pour concrete to columns						‖	‖													

52

7. Fix steel to ringbeam	8. Fix formwork to ringbeam	9. Pour concrete to ringbeam	10. Fabricate and fix roof trusses	11. Tile roof	12. Fit infill panels	13. Fix ceiling	14. Fit and glaze windows	15. Paint	16. Clear site

PROGRAMME SITUATION AT THE END OF WEEK 14 (FOUR WEEKS BEHIND SCHEDULE)

BAR CHART - CONSTRUCTION PHASE

Item	Week number																			
	01	02	03	04	05	06	07	08	09	10	11	12	13	14	15	16	17	18	19	20
1. Excavate foundations	▮	▮																		
2. Fix steel foundations		▮	▮																	
3. Pour concrete to foundations				▮																
4. Fix steel to columns				▮	▮															
5. Fix formwork to columns					▮	▮														
6. Pour concrete to columns						▮	▮													

7. Fix steel to ringbeam

8. Fix formwork to ringbeam

9. Pour concrete to ringbeam

10. Fabricate and fix roof trusses

11. Tile roof

12. Fit infill panels

13. Fix ceiling

14. Fit and glaze windows

15. Paint

16. Clear site

Item	Week number																			
	01	02	03	04	05	06	07	08	09	10	11	12	13	14	15	16	17	18	19	20
1. Excavate foundations																				
2. Fix steel foundations																				
3. Pour concrete to foundations																				
4. Fix steel to columns																				
5. Fix formwork to columns																				
6. Pour concrete to columns																				

56

7. Fix steel to ringbeam

8. Fix formwork to ringbeam

9. Pour concrete to ringbeam

10. Fabricate and fix roof trusses

11. Tile roof

12. Fit infill panels

13. Fix ceiling

14. Fit and glaze windows

15. Paint

16. Clear site

BAR CHART - FEEDER ROADS A, B AND C

Section A

Item	Month number 01	02	03	04	05	06	07	08	09	10	11	12	13	14	15
1. Road A km 0-2	▓	▓													
2. Road A km 2-4			▓	▓											
3. Road B km 0-2					▓	▓									
4. Road B km 2-4						▒		│							
5. Road B km 4-6								▒		│					
6. Road C km 0-2									▒		│				
7. Road C km 2-4									▒				│		
8. Road C km 4-5									▒					│	│

Section B

Item	Month number														
	01	02	03	04	05	06	07	08	09	10	11	12	13	14	15
1. Road A km 0-2															
2. Road A km 2-4															
3. Road B km 0-2															
4. Road B km 2-4															
5. Road B km 4-6															
6. Road C km 0-2															
7. Road C km 2-4															
8. Road C km 4-5															

Now check your answers

Our answers are at the end of this workbook. We suggest you check your answers against them before deciding on your action programme. If there is any disagreement, re-read Chapter 7 of the handbook to make sure you fully understand it.

Part 3 - Action programme

How to construct your action programme

Parts 1 and 2 should have helped you to recognize your strengths and weaknesses as the owner or manager of a construction enterprise. The general questions in Part 1 are a good guide to the strengths of your business and also to the areas where there is most room for improvement. So look back and count the number of times you answered "yes" or "no".

How many times did you answer "yes"? The more "yes" answers, the more likely it is that your business will do well. Now look again at those questions where you answered "no". These may be problem or opportunity areas for your business. Choose the one which is most important at the present time. This is the sensible way to improve your business. Take the most urgent problem first. Don't try to solve everything at once.

Now write the problem or opportunity into the following action programme, as we have done with the example. Then write in <u>What must be done</u>, <u>By whom</u> and <u>By when</u> in order to make sure things improve.

Finally, go back to your business and carry out the action programme.

Problem	What must be done	By whom?	By when?
When a project falls behind schedule it is very difficult to bring it back	(a) Discuss the problem with the site foremen. Remember, they may have ideas I have not thought of (b) Discuss the problem with the consultant and ask for advice. Never hide the problem or hope for the best	Self	As soon as the problem shows up on the bar chart

PART B
MAKING IT HAPPEN

SUPERVISION 8

Quick reference

- ❏ All projects need efficient supervision.
- ❏ An efficient site supervision can ensure that a project is executed without cost or time overruns.
- ❏ Supervisors need to have authority to match their responsibility – never criticize them in front of other staff.
- ❏ Supervisors need to know exactly who and what they are responsible for – and who they themselves answer to.

REMEMBER

- ❏ The supervisor must be respected by the workers and be a good communicator.
- ❏ The supervisor must be able to plan the next day's and the next week's work.
- ❏ The supervisor must be able to read the bar chart and schedules.
- ❏ The supervisor and the contractor should trust each other.
- ❏ The supervisor should help to ensure a good relationship between the workers and the contractor.
- ❏ There should be an incentive, perhaps in the form of a bonus, for the site managers and foremen to perform well.
- ❏ The supervisor must be given authority to match responsibility.
- ❏ Always inform the supervisors and workers of change to come.
- ❏ Problems should not be ignored since they will not go away.
- ❏ List the problems, then deal with them one by one.
- ❏ Tackle the worst problem first. It may be that solving it will help towards solving the rest.
- ❏ Do not be afraid to ask for suggestions.

Part 1 – Questions

	Yes	No
1. Do you try to recruit – and keep – good supervisors?	☐	☐
2. Do you trust your supervisors?	☐	☐
3. Do you believe you are trusted by your supervisors?	☐	☐
4. Do you make sure that salaries and wages are paid on time?	☐	☐
5. Do you try not to lose your temper when things go wrong?	☐	☐
6. Do you listen to advice from your supervisors and workers?	☐	☐
7. Do you know all your workers by name?	☐	☐
8. Do you help your workers to improve their skills?	☐	☐
9. Do you do your best to reduce accidents on site?	☐	☐
10. Do you believe you have a reputation as a good employer?	☐	☐

Part 2 – Business practice

Exercise 1   RECRUITING A SITE AGENT

You have been awarded a new contract.

The tender sum is 1,000,000 NU – before profit (i.e. what it costs you as a contractor to complete the contract).

The project period is two years.

You have to recruit a new site agent to manage the project, and have received three applications from experienced agents. Having checked their references, you can make a reasonable guess as to how well they are likely to perform.

❑ Site agent A demands a salary of 20,000 NU per year. He would be able to keep the project cost to 1,000,000 NU.

❑ Site agent B demands a salary of 30,000 NU per year. Because he is more skilled than A, he can probably save you 1 per cent of the project cost.

❑ Site agent C demands a salary of 40,000 NU per year. Because he is very highly skilled, he can probably save you 5 per cent of the project cost.

Which of the three site agents would you recruit for the contract?

Exercise 2   MONDAY'S PROBLEMS

You have been away from your site for two weeks attending an Improve Your Construction Business seminar. On your return (Monday 7 a.m.) you find that your foreman has left on your desk the following list of problems that he could not handle himself.

A. The concrete test cube taken on the foundation pour has failed on a seven-day test. The masons are waiting for the go-ahead to start on the blockwork to floor level.

B. The concrete mixer has broken down. It will take two weeks to repair and a large payment has to be made in advance.

C. Only one load of blocks has arrived, but the main delivery is expected tomorrow.

D. The Minister of Works has suddenly decided to visit the site on Wednesday. He will stay for a barbecue lunch (which will be provided by the consultant), but the consultant has sent a written instruction to build a temporary shaded area where the meal can be served.

E. Your payment for the last but one certificate measurement (presented to the client two months ago) is going to be delayed for a further two months, according to the chief accountant at the Ministry of Works, but you need the money NOW.

What are you going to do about solving these problems?

Now check your answers

Our suggested answers are at the end of this workbook. We suggest that you check your answers against them before deciding on your action programme. If there is any disagreement, re-read Chapter 8 of the handbook to make sure you fully understand it.

Part 3 – Action programme

How to construct your action programme

Parts 1 and 2 should have helped you to recognize your strengths and weaknesses as the owner or manager of a construction enterprise. The general questions in Part 1 are a good guide to the strengths of your business and also to the areas where there is most room for improvement. So look back and count the number of times you answered "yes" or "no".

How many times did you answer "yes"? The more "yes" answers, the more likely it is that your business will do well. Now look again at those questions where you answered "no". These may be problem or opportunity areas for your business. Choose the one which is most important at the present time. This is the sensible way to improve your business. Take the most urgent problem first. Don't try to solve everything at once.

Now write the problem or opportunity into the following action programme, as we have done with the example. Then write in <u>What must be done</u>, <u>By whom</u> and <u>By when</u> in order to make sure things improve.

Finally, go back to your business and carry out the action programme.

Problem	What must be done	By whom?	By when?
There have been a series of small accidents at Site A	Discuss the cause of each of the accidents with the site foreman and other workers. Prepare an accident prevention programme with them before a serious accident happens	Site team	Monday morning

SITE LAYOUT 9

Quick reference

Make a site layout plan before work starts

A spare copy of the site plan can be used for deciding the best layout. The plan should show all the buildings to be constructed, their foundations, drainage and service runs, roads and paths. Then the best location for materials, equipment, huts, specialist work areas are decided by trial and error. You can use a pencil and rubber, cardboard cut-outs to the same scale, or a plastic overlay and crayons. Once the best solution has been found, draw it out clearly, and show it to everyone who is likely to need the information. Remember that errors made on paper do not cost you money, whereas errors made on site can be very expensive.

REMEMBER

❑ Good site layout saves time and money.

❑ An untidy workplace is often the main reason for accidents.

❑ The selected layout must give easy access for all deliveries and other transport.

❑ You need a list of all the items to be positioned on site and an indication of how they will be transported to and from the site.

❑ A site layout plan is one of the most essential elements in a successful project.

Part 1 - Questions

		Yes	No
1.	Do you always make a site layout plan before work starts?	☐	☐
2.	Do you think carefully about where to put the access road?	☐	☐
3.	Do you think carefully about where to put the cement shed and stores?	☐	☐
4.	Do you make sure that your aggregate stockpile and concrete mixer are placed close to where the concrete and mortar will be needed?	☐	☐
5.	Do you make sure that bricks and blocks are placed so as to avoid double handling?	☐	☐
6.	Do you make sure that clean water is available on the site?	☐	☐
7.	Do you know how to cut handling and stacking time?	☐	☐
8.	Do you know how to use site planning to reduce the distances that materials and workers have to travel?	☐	☐
9.	Do you know if the materials on your sites are well stacked for ease of storage and handling? . . .	☐	☐
10.	Do you always make sure that the site office is positioned so that it gives a clear view of the site?	☐	☐

Part 2 - Business practice

Exercise 1   A BAD SITE LAYOUT?

The plan on page 72 shows the site layout for the construction of a radio transmitter station on a remote site in open country.
What are your criticisms of the layout? Can you find 15 possible faults? What are they?

1. ....

2. ....

3. ....

4. ....

5. ....

6. ....

7. ....

8. ....

9. ....

10. ....

11. ....

12. ....

13. ....

14. ....

15. ....

Exercise 2   YOUR TURN

If you were in charge of the construction work, where would you locate the various items of equipment, storage, work areas, etc., at the very start of the job?

Show your layout on the blank site plan.

Figure 1. Layout of site for construction of a radio transmitter station.

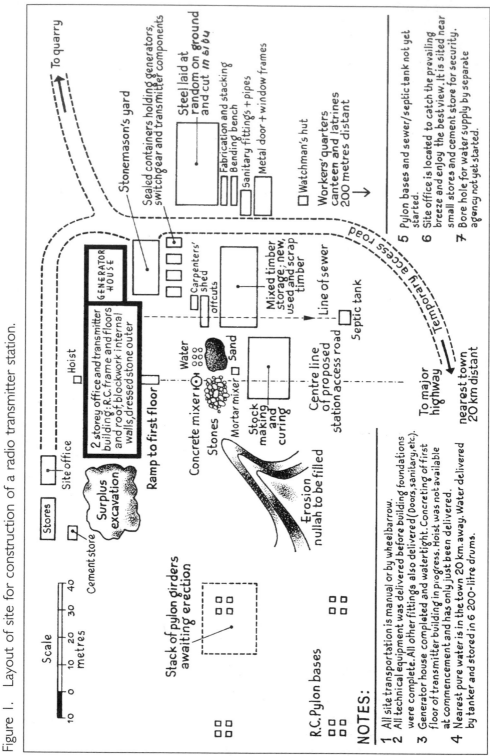

Figure 2. Blank site plan

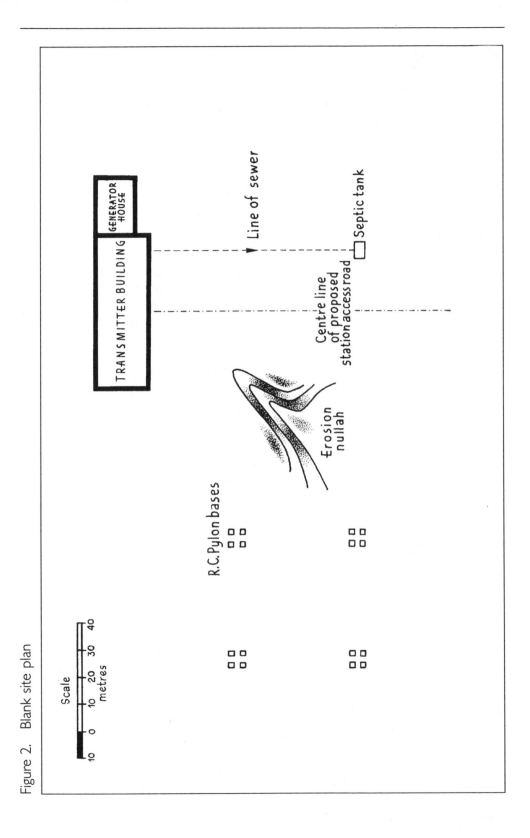

Our answers are at the end of this workbook. We suggest you check your answers against them before deciding on your action programme. If there is any disagreement, re-read Chapter 9 of the handbook to make sure you fully understand it.

Part 3 - Action programme

How to construct your action programme

Parts 1 and 2 should have helped you to recognize your strengths and weaknesses as the owner or manager of a construction enterprise. The general questions in Part 1 are a good guide to the strengths of your business and also to the areas where there is most room for improvement. So look back and count the number of times you answered "yes" or "no".

How many times did you answer "yes"? The more "yes" answers, the more likely it is that your business will do well. Now look again at those questions where you answered "no". These may be problem or opportunity areas for your business. Choose the one which is most important at the present time. This is the sensible way to improve your business. Take the most urgent problem first. Don't try to solve everything at once.

Now write the problem or opportunity into the action programme opposite, as we have done with the example. Then write in <u>What must be done</u>, <u>By whom</u> and <u>By when</u> in order to make sure things improve.

Finally, go back to your business and carry out the action programme.

Problem	What must be done	By whom?	By when?
The last project lost money due to double handling of materials	Before the next project starts, there must be a plan for a good site layout to ensure that materials are placed close to where they will be needed and that they do not interfere with other operations	Self and foreman	Before start of site work

WHAT IS PRODUCTIVITY?   10

Quick reference

❑ Productivity on a site is a measure of the time workers and plant are active and efficient, so that they earn money for your business.

❑ In order to maintain a high rate of productivity it is necessary to plan, organize, control and coordinate all project activities.

❑ It is necessary to spend time inspecting your current work methods so as to improve them.

REMEMBER

❑ Higher productivity means getting <u>more output</u> for <u>less input</u>, i.e. <u>lower</u> <u>cost</u> or <u>less time</u> to produce the same amount.

❑ Productivity covers every activity on a construction site, workshop or fabrication yard.

❑ A high activity level means that the workers are kept busy doing productive things that contribute to completing the project in the most efficient way.

❑ By observing any operation the entrepreneur can work out ways to change it in order to improve productivity.

❑ Higher productivity means higher profits.

Part 1 - Questions

1. Do you regularly check the activity level on
   your sites? . . . .   ☐   ☐

2. Do you train your supervisors in ways
   to improve productivity? . . . .   ☐   ☐

3. Do you make sure that your workers
   have good tools? . . . .   ☐   ☐

4. Do you make sure that materials are always
   available when and where they are needed? . . . . .   ☐   ☐

5. Do you make sure that workers are never kept
   waiting for instructions? . . . .   ☐   ☐

6. Do you plan carefully so that workers do not get
   in each other's way? . . . .   ☐   ☐

7. Do you regularly look at site operations and ask
   yourself if there is a better way? . . . .   ☐   ☐

8. Do you ask other contractors for advice when
   you feel that productivity could be improved? . . . .   ☐   ☐

9. Do you discuss productivity with your supervisors? .   ☐   ☐

10. Do your supervisors discuss productivity with
    your workers? . . . .   ☐   ☐

Part 2 - Business practice

Exercise 1   WHAT A SITE!

You have taken on a new foreman and are visiting the site to see
how he is getting on. The sketch on the following page shows
the strip footing ready to receive concrete.

The centre of the building site has been stripped of soil con-
taining vegetable matter, leaving a very muddy area to be filled
with hardcore. The excavation from the centre and from the
footings has been piled around the outside of the trench and an
opening has been made through the excavated material for
access. Planks have been laid to allow one-way access for wheelbarrows. There is no room to walk between the trench and the
excavated material.

One labourer works behind the mixer to load sand, stone and cement. The mixer operator controls the water by filling buckets from the bowser, which cannot be moved closer than 4 m from the mixer.

The trench and reinforcing steel ahead of the concrete are cleaned out where excavated material has fallen in. This is done by two labourers, one to lift the steel and one to clean out the soil.

The placing gang consists of two: one to spread and one on the vibrator.

The mixer can serve three wheelbarrows, so three labourers deliver the concrete.

The pour has just started:

A. Describe any problems that you would point out to your foreman.

B. What should have been done to stop those problems occurring?

C. What would you do now to improve the productivity of this operation?

Figure 4. Plan of strip footing

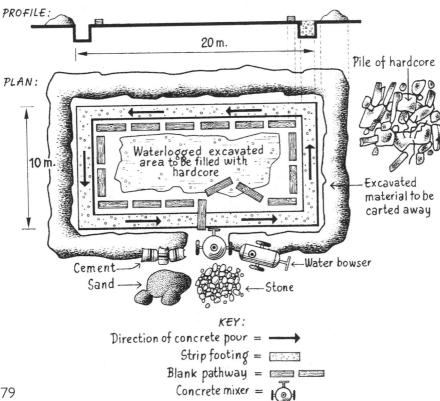

PROFILE:

20 m.

Pile of hardcore

PLAN:

10 m.

Waterlogged excavated area to be filled with hardcore

Excavated material to be carted away

Cement

Sand

Stone

Water bowser

KEY:

Direction of concrete pour = →

Strip footing =

Blank pathway =

Concrete mixer =

79

Exercise 2   CUTTING COSTS

Your next visit is to your sand pit, where you have deposits for another 12 months.

Figure 5.
Stockpiling sand

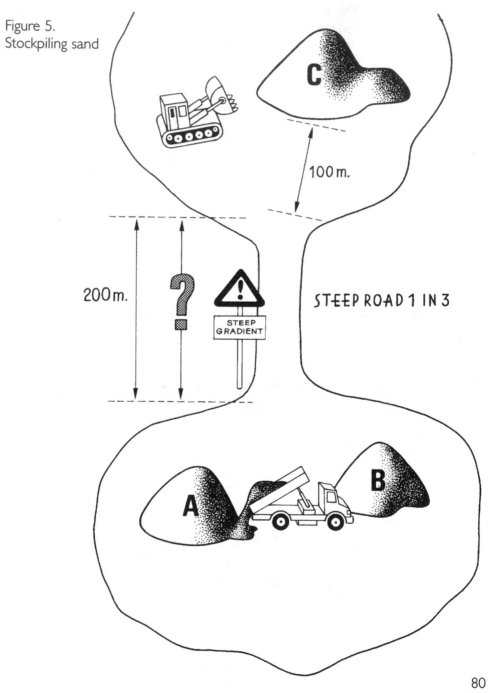

C

100 m.

200 m.

?

⚠
STEEP
GRADIENT

STEEP ROAD 1 IN 3

A

B

Figure 5 shows a front-end loader stockpiling sand to stockpile C. The truck stops at stockpiles A and B because it cannot climb the very steep access road when full. In order to get the sand from C to A and B, 40 labourers have been hired on a permanent basis to barrow the sand up the steep road.

A. What are the main problems that you face?

B. Can costs be cut without reducing output? (In other words - can productivity be improved?)

C. How can this be done?

Now check your answers

Our answers are at the end of this workbook. We suggest you check your answers against them before deciding on your action programme. If there is any disagreement, re-read Chapter 10 of the handbook to make sure you fully understand it.

Part 3 - Action programme

How to construct your action programme

Parts 1 and 2 should have helped you to recognize your strengths and weaknesses as the owner or manager of a construction enterprise. The general questions in Part 1 are a good guide to the strengths of your business and also to the areas where there is most room for improvement. So look back and count the number of times you answered "yes" or "no".

How many times did you answer "yes"? The more "yes" answers, the more likely it is that your business will do well. Now look again at those questions where you answered "no". These may be problem or opportunity areas for your business. Choose the one which is most important at the present time. This is the sensible way to improve your business. Take the most urgent problem first. Don't try to solve everything at once.

Now write the problem or opportunity into the action programme on the next page, as we have done with the example. Then write in <u>What must be done</u>, <u>By whom</u> and <u>By when</u> in order to make sure things improve.

Finally, go back to your business and carry out the action programme.

Problem	What must be done	By whom?	By when?
Output on the site of the primary school is only half what I expected	Spend a day on site with the foreman and check the productivity of all main operations	Self/ foreman	Next Tuesday

IMPROVING WORK METHODS 11

Quick reference

- ❏ Productivity improvement is not so much a method as a way of thinking.
- ❏ Productivity can be increased by improving work methods.

REMEMBER

- ❏ When productivity is improved, money is saved. Raised productivity means raised profits.
- ❏ Improved productivity can improve the conditions of the workers.
- ❏ By improving the work method the cost of an operation can be reduced.
- ❏ By improving the work method the time taken to complete the operation can be reduced.
- ❏ There are four steps to improving the work method: select the job operation; record and describe the present method; improve the method; install the new method.
- ❏ Low activity could be due to bad planning and bad organization.
- ❏ The workforce cannot be expected to work full out, all the time-rests are needed to maintain efficient working.
- ❏ Each job should be planned, controlled and reorganized if necessary.
- ❏ If the <u>actual</u> activity level is <u>lower</u> than your estimated (average) activity level, then money is <u>lost</u>.
- ❏ If the <u>actual</u> activity level is <u>higher</u> than your estimated (average) activity level, then money is <u>made</u>.

Part I - Questions

		Yes	No

1. Do you frequently take time to walk around your site, looking at the operations going on and planning better ways of getting things done?..... ☐ ☐

2. Do you know how productive your workers are when you are not on site to watch them?....... ☐ ☐

3. Do you make sure that your foremen understand how to run a productive site?................. ☐ ☐

4. Do you make sure that you always have a true picture of what is happening on your sites?...... ☐ ☐

5. Do you make sure that you, as a manager, set a good example in improving work methods?..... ☐ ☐

6. Do you know that your workers need not work harder in order to work more efficiently?....... ☐ ☐

7. Do you know when a worker is only pretending to be more productive by skimping on quality standards?............................... ☐ ☐

8. Do you know how to find the reasons for low activity?............................... ☐ ☐

9. Do you know how to calculate the costs of alternative production methods?.............. ☐ ☐

10. Do you believe that there are always possibilities of making every site more productive?........ ☐ ☐

Part 2 - Business practice

Exercise 1   WORKING BETTER

Consider how you would go about improving the work method on the following job.

The site layout on the next page (figure 6) shows a small joiner's workshop and yard. The owner has won a contract to supply a new housing site with roof trusses, and realizes that the workshop and yard will be so congested that there will not be enough space available to store the finished trusses prior to collection. You visit the premises and find that:

❏   The joiner's main task is to supervise the jobs.

❏   Two carpenters and two labourers are employed on an hourly basis – they can start and finish when they like.

❏   Timber is stacked wherever there is room, and deliveries are haphazard.

❏   One carpenter makes furniture for sale – this is a money-maker for the entrepreneur, yielding modest but regular profit.

❏   One carpenter works on contract jobs when they occur.

❏   When the carpenters need a length of timber they get it themselves, measuring random lengths until they find the right size.

❏   The length of timber is then worked by the carpenter.

❏   The finished articles are stacked wherever room can be found. Furniture has to be locked in the workshop at night.

❏   The owner cannot be on the site the whole time due to other managerial duties.

❏   The owner also has a haulage business, and owns a flat truck.

❏   The client's site is ten miles away.

❏   The contract will be signed in a week's time, when the job must start.

Figure 6. Site layout for joiner's workshop and yard

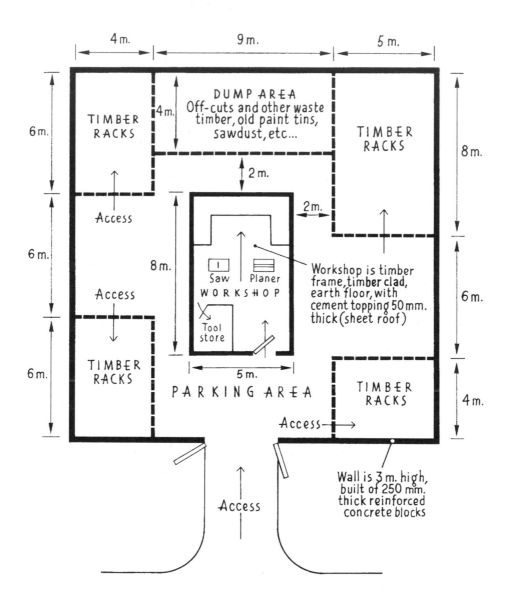

Now check your answers

Our answers are at the end of this workbook. We suggest you check your answers against them before deciding on your action programme. If there is any disagreement, re-read Chapter 11 of the handbook to make sure you fully understand it.

Part 3 - Action programme

How to construct your action programme

Parts 1 and 2 should have helped you to recognize your strengths and weaknesses as the owner or manager of a construction enterprise. The general questions in Part 1 are a good guide to the strengths of your business and also to the areas where there is most room for improvement. So look back and count the number of times you answered "yes" or "no".

How many times did you answer "yes"? The more "yes" answers, the more likely it is that your business will do well. Now look again at those questions where you answered "no". These may be problem or opportunity areas for your business. Choose the one which is most important at the present time. This is the sensible way to improve your business. Take the most urgent problem first. Don't try to solve everything at once.

Now write the problem or opportunity into the action programme opposite, as we have done with the example. Then write in <u>What must be done</u>, <u>By whom</u> and <u>By when</u> in order to make sure things improve.

Finally, go back to your business and carry out the action programme.

Problem	What must be done	By whom?	By when?
It is not easy to find a way to improve work methods	Use the four steps: *select* the job/operation *record* and describe the present method of doing the job *improve* the method by thinking of better ways to do the job *install* the improved method on the job	Site team	Start tomorrow

INCENTIVE SCHEMES 12

Quick reference

❏ Incentive schemes can be an effective way of improving productivity.

❏ Successful contractors tend to pay their workers quite well and at the same time do well in business.

REMEMBER

❏ Effective payment schemes can lead to higher profits and increased efficiency.

❏ The most common methods of payment are:

daily (or hourly) wage

piecework

taskwork

bonus schemes

❏ Payment schemes introduced to improve productivity should be carefully prepared and administered.

Part 1 - Questions

		Yes	No
1.	Do you always look for ways to reward workers for good work?	☐	☐
2.	Do you believe that incentive schemes can increase productivity?	☐	☐
3.	Do you make sure that you give your workers incentives to work harder and better whenever possible?.	☐	☐
4.	Do you understand the term "piecework"?.	☐	☐
5.	Do you understand how a bonus system works?.	☐	☐
6.	Do you believe that the system used for paying your workers can have a major impact on the efficiency of your site?.	☐	☐
7.	Do you know that successful contractors usually pay their workers well, and also earn good profits?.	☐	☐
8.	Do you understand the term "taskwork"?.	☐	☐
9.	Do you know the difference between the terms "piecework", "taskwork" and "bonus schemes"?. .	☐	☐
10.	Do you think an incentive scheme for paying workers could lead to better site productivity than a fixed daily wage?	☐	☐

Part 2 - Business practice

Exercise 1   CHOOSE YOUR METHOD!

Four very different operations are described below. For each operation:

A. Describe the method of payment you would use.

B. Explain why you would use the method.

C. Describe how you would organize the administration (supervision) of the method.

OPERATION 1. A team of 20 labourers and a foreman are to excavate 300 m of foundation trenches.

OPERATION 2. The finishings are to be done inside a building by a team consisting of two masons and two carpenters. At the same time, electricians and plumbers from other companies are working there to finish off their operations.

OPERATION 3. The reinforced concrete floor slab, including a complex network of cable ducts, for an electronics laboratory is to be constructed to a high standard of precision. The alignment, positioning and gradient of the channels must all accurately reflect the drawings. The job will take three weeks for two masons and four labourers.

OPERATION 4. Three external staircases are to be constructed in concrete for a two-storey building. They are to be curved. It is the first time you have been faced with this kind of job. Two highly skilled carpenters with helpers are to be employed to fix the formwork, and two masons with helpers will mix and pour the concrete.

Now check your answers

Our answers are at the end of this workbook. We suggest you check your answers against them before deciding on your action programme. If there is any disagreement, re-read Chapter 12 of the handbook to make sure you fully understand it.

Part 3 - Action programme

How to construct your action programme

Parts 1 and 2 should have helped you to recognize your strengths and weaknesses as the owner or manager of a construction enterprise. The general questions in Part 1 are a good guide to the strengths of your business and also to the areas where there is most room for improvement. So look back and count the number of times you answered "yes" or "no".

How many times did you answer "yes"? The more "yes" answers, the more likely it is that your business will do well. Now look again at those questions where you answered "no". These may be problem or opportunity areas for your business. Choose the one which is most important at the present time. This is the sensible way to improve your business. Take the most urgent problem first. Don't try to solve everything at once.

Now write the problem or opportunity into the action programme below, as we have done with the example. Then write in <u>What must be done</u>, <u>By whom</u> and <u>By when</u> in order to make sure things improve.

Finally, go back to your business and carry out the action programme

Problem	What must be done	By whom?	By when?
My workers do not seem to care about improving productivity	Decide carefully on output targets and the scope for saving money through better productivity, and introduce an incentive scheme	Self and site team	One month to discuss and prepare

HEALTH AND SAFETY   13

Quick reference

❑ Make sure that you enforce safety regulations at all times.

❑ You must always do your best to protect the occupational health and safety of the workforce.

❑ You can actually increase your profits by taking adequate steps to avoid additional costs incurred through accidents on the site or job-related illness.

REMEMBER

❑ You as a contractor are ultimately responsible for enforcing safety regulations.

❑ A planned accident-prevention programme can cut down on time lost through injury and job-related illness.

❑ Accidents can be expensive to you, but an accident-prevention programme can cut costs.

❑ The contractor is responsible for making the workforce aware of risks.

❑ Every accident has a cause. If hazards can be detected then accidents can be prevented.

❑ You should ensure that the workforce carry out their tasks in a safe and healthy working environment.

Part 1 - Questions

	Yes	No
1. Do you always make sure that new workers realize the risks if they ignore safety procedures? .	☐	☐
2. Do you make regular safety checks on your sites?	☐	☐
3. Do you make sure that your workers are supplied with – and use – safety equipment?.	☐	☐
4. Do you allow for safety costs in your bids?	☐	☐
5. Do you allow for safety measures when preparing job plans?.	☐	☐
6. Do you understand that unsafe working practices damage your profits?.	☐	☐
7. Do you know that large construction firms often have entire units devoted to preventing accidents and job-related illnesses?.	☐	☐
8. Do you have an accident-prevention programme?.	☐	☐
9. Do you set an example by wearing a safety helmet when you walk around your sites?	☐	☐
10. Do you talk about safety performance as well as output whenever you discuss progress with your site foremen?.	☐	☐

Part 2 - Business practice

Exercise 1   YOU ARE A SAFETY INSPECTOR!

In this exercise you should imagine that you are a safety inspec-
tor, and that you have been called in to investigate and report
on two accidents. This will mean filling in the following details on
the accident report forms:

Injury   A brief description of how the person involved
              was hurt

Accident   A brief description of what happened

Cause   The reasons for the accident, stating physical
              causes rather than personal negligence

Responsibility Note all cases of negligence by people involved in
              the accident, both directly (those on the spot)
              and indirectly (those responsible for the work
              environment).

Case 1   The circular saw

An experienced carpenter was given the task of trimming the
edges of a batch of moulded timber panels. His supervisor
suggested that he save time by using a portable electric circular
saw. As he had very seldom used one before, he decided to use
a hand saw instead – but the result was poor.

He went to the other end of the workshop to borrow the
portable saw, and on his return placed it on top of a batch of
panels while he plugged the lead into the nearest electric
socket. The lead was not long enough to reach the socket, so
he went back to the other end of the workshop to borrow an
extension lead.

When he got back, he plugged the extension lead into the
socket. Then he walked to the batch of panels on which the
portable saw was resting and started to connect the plug of the
saw onto the socket of the extension lead. As soon as the
connection was made, the saw began to rotate. It came off the
panels and struck the man on his left arm, causing a severe cut.

Following the accident, it was discovered that the socket
switch had been in the "on" position, and the carpenter had not
noticed this. The trigger switch on the portable tool was held
down with adhesive tape so that it was permanently in the "on"
position. Further investigation showed that this tape had been
applied when the saw had been mounted on a fixed bench
some time previously. Further investigation revealed that the
spring-loaded guard on the lower part of the saw was jammed
in the open position. Thus almost half the blade was permanently exposed. All these defects had existed for at least a
month in spite of a system of checks which was supposed to be
in operation.

A deep cut in the top panel of the batch showed that when the current was connected, the saw had dug into the panel and the speed of rotation had caused it to be thrown off the top of the batch of panels.

ACCIDENT REPORT	CASE 1: THE CIRCULAR SAW
Injury	
Accident	
Cause	
Responsibility	

Case 2   The labourer and the ladder

A manager in a warehouse had visited the dispatch department (see figure 8 on the following page) to check on the progress of an urgent order. He was in a bad temper and, as he was about to leave, he told the foreman that the department had to be cleaned up. He particularly pointed out the dirt on the top of the pipes and on the ledge. Next he drew the foreman's attention to the dirty cartons on top of the partitioned office. They had obviously been there for some time. "Get that junk down, as well" he shouted.

When the manager had left, the foreman told the labourer to clean up the department "and be quick about it".

The labourer collected the ladder which was kept in the department, since it was of a convenient length to reach both the ledge and the service pipes.

No other ladder was readily available in the department, but other ladders of different lengths were available elsewhere.

The labourer propped the ladder against the ledge, at a safe angle, and cleaned the ledge and the pipes. However, he did not wedge it, nor was he instructed to do so. There was no-one else around who could hold the foot of the ladder.

The labourer then needed to reach the cartons, and moved the ladder across to rest on the edge of the partition. Because the ceiling was lower in that part of the department, it was not possible to set the ladder at the correct angle. He climbed up the ladder to remove the cartons. As he was coming down with them in his arms, the ladder slipped along the metal floor. The labourer could not save himself from falling and his right wrist was fractured.

Now check your answers

Our answers are at the end of this workbook. We suggest you check your answers against them before deciding on your action programme. If there is any disagreement, re-read Chapter 13 of the handbook to make sure you fully understand it.

Figure 8. Dispatch department accident

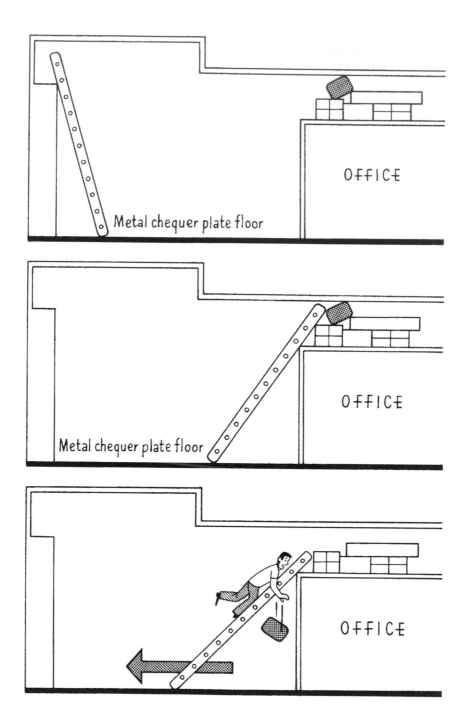

ACCIDENT REPORT	CASE 2: THE LABOURER AND THE LADDER
Injury	
Accident	
Cause	
Responsibility	

Part 3 - Action programme

How to construct your action programme

Parts 1 and 2 should have helped you to recognize your strengths and weaknesses as the owner or manager of a construction enterprise. The general questions in Part 1 are a good guide to the strengths of your business and also to the areas where there is most room for improvement. So look back and count the number of times you answered "yes" or "no".

How many times did you answer "yes"? The more "yes" answers, the more likely it is that your business will do well. Now look again at those questions where you answered "no". These may be problem or opportunity areas for your business. Choose the one which is most important at the present time. This is the sensible way to improve your business. Take the most urgent problem first. Don't try to solve everything at once.

Now write the problem or opportunity into the action programme below, as we have done with the example. Then write in <u>What must be done</u>, <u>By whom</u> and <u>By when</u> in order to make sure things improve.

Finally, go back to your business and carry out the action programme.

Problem	What must be done	By whom?	By when?
I cannot afford to buy safety wear and equipment for my workers	Accidents on site cost me time and money so I must find a way to afford safety equipment, even if it means delaying other purchases 1. I will defer other purchases and buy safety equipment now 2. I will allow for safety costs in my next bid	 Self Self/ quantity surveyor	 Now Next bid

QUALITY CONTROL   14

Quick reference

❏ An effective system of quality control can detect unacceptable work before it is too late.

❏ You should make an effort to develop and sustain your own system of quality control.

❏ An effective system of quality control means money saved.

REMEMBER

❏ A system of quality control makes it easier for the contractor to achieve the required standards.

❏ A system of quality control can save the contractor money.

❏ A system of quality control can lead to better relations with the client and the client's representatives.

❏ The better the quality control, the better the finished product.

❏ You should never accept materials that are substandard.

❏ Good supervision means good quality control.

Part 1 - Questions

	Yes	No
1. Do you always check materials delivered to site and reject any items which are below specification?	☐	☐
2. Do you know what percentage of your materials is wasted through bad workmanship?	☐	☐
3. Do you make sure that faulty work is put right immediately?	☐	☐
4. Do you make sure that the mixer operator never adds more water than is specified in the mix design?	☐	☐
5. Do you make sure that you always provide your suppliers with exact specifications?	☐	☐
6. Do you check on the quality of sand, aggregates, concrete blocks and other basic materials at their source?	☐	☐
7. Do you know and apply all the simple tests of materials that can be done on site?	☐	☐
8. Do you know how to make a concrete test cube correctly?	☐	☐
9. Do you know how to make a concrete slump test correctly?	☐	☐
10. Do you have a system of quality control on your sites?	☐	☐

Part 2 - Business practice

Exercise 1   QUALITY CONTROL

What methods would you use on site to control the quality and accuracy of the following jobs? Prepare five sketches to illustrate your answers.

A. Straight alignment and accurate width of strip footings

B. Accurate levels of an excavation

C. Laying of drainage pipes to correct fall

D. Alignment of pipes after laying and before backfill

E. Correct standard width of joints in bathroom tiles.

Exercise 2   THE ROOF COLLAPSES

A builder buys a quantity of ten substandard lintels from a manufacturer/supplier. The builder does not test them and the supplier does not give a warranty with them. They are delivered to site, and although one is dropped while being off-loaded and broken, the builder still accepts the other nine (there is no charge for the broken lintel). The clerk of works looks at them and does not condemn them, but he does not accept them in writing either, and they are built in to the works.

Three months later the lintels crack in half and the roof collapses:

❏ Who is to blame, and why?

❏ Who must pay for what?

NOW CHECK YOUR ANSWERS

Our answers are at the end of this workbook. We suggest you check your answers against them before deciding on your action programme. If there is any disagreement, re-read Chapter 14 of the handbook to make sure you fully understand it.

103

Part 3 - Action programme

How to construct your action programme

Parts 1 and 2 should have helped you to recognize your strengths and weaknesses as the owner or manager of a construction enterprise. The general questions in Part 1 are a good guide to the strengths of your business and also to the areas where there is most room for improvement. So look back and count the number of times you answered "yes" or "no".

How many times did you answer "yes"? The more "yes" answers, the more likely it is that your business will do well. Now look again at those questions where you answered "no". These may be problem or opportunity areas for your business. Choose the one which is most important at the present time. This is the sensible way to improve your business. Take the most urgent problem first. Don't try to solve everything at once.

Now write the problem or opportunity into the action programme below, as we have done with the example. Then write in <u>What must be done</u>, <u>By whom</u> and <u>By when</u> in order to make sure things improve.

Finally, go back to your business and carry out the action programme.

Problem	What must be done	By whom?	By when?
The Clerk of Works is rejecting a lot of work that the site staff considered satisfactory	1. Make sure that the site staff are familiar with the specifications	Site staff/self	Five days
	2. Meet all site staff and encourage them to pay more attention to the quality of work	Self	Ten days
	3. Consider giving a monthly bonus to staff on sites where no work is rejected	Self	Two weeks
	4. Instruct all foremen that faulty work must be put right immediately	Self	Now

Answers to business practice - 1

Exercise 1   HOW TO DO IT

Job	Mostly labour	Mostly equipment (state type)
1. Site clearance – removal of light undergrowth	×	
2. Strip topsoil		Grader/loader/
	tipper truck	
3. Excavate strip foundations	×	
4. Bulk fill to road base		Dozer/loader/
	tipper/roller	
5. Rural feeder road construction	×	
6. Mix concrete for house floors		Mixer
7. Place concrete for house floors	×	
8. Place mass concrete fill		Dumper
9. Place timber roof trusses to houses	×	
10. Place steel roof trusses to factory workshops		Crane
11. Build brick walls	×	
12. Build concrete block walls	×	
13. Place precast concrete wall panels		Crane
14. Excavate trenches 1.5 - 2.0 metres deep		Backhoe
15. Bed, lay and haunch sewer pipes	×	

Answers to business practice - 2

Exercise 1 COMPLETE THE ALLOWABLES

ALLOWABLES CHART

Item no.	Description	Unit	Cost allowables			Time allowables		
			Labour	Plant	Transport	Labour	Plant	Transport
2.	Steel to foundations	tonne	263		7	10.1 days		
3.	Formwork to foundations	m²	2.9	-	0.2	0.11 days		
5.	Steel to columns	tonne	441		8	17.0 days		
6.	Formwork to columns	m²	2.1		0.1	0.08 days		
7.	Concrete to columns	m³	30.3	8.6	4.9	0.54 days		
8.	Block walls up to floor	m²	2.9		0.9	0.09 days		
10.	Hardcore fill	m³	4.9	1.4	0.6	0.18 days		
11.	Mesh to floor	tonne	400		8	15.4 days		
12.	Concrete to floor	m³	24.7	7.1	4.6	0.44 days		
13.	Block walls above floor	m²	2.7		1.0	0.09 days		
17.	Steel to ringbeam	tonne	520		13	20.0 days		
18.	Concrete to ringbeam	m³	43.1	12.3	4.1	0.77 days		

The calculations given on the next few pages show how we arrived at the figures in each row of the Allowables chart on the previous page:

2. Steel to foundations

Since we have different dimensions of reinforcement we need to look at allowables per tonne of steel instead of per metre.

12 mm weighs 0.89 kg/m and 8 mm weighs 0.40 kg/m.

That gives us: $(300 \times 0.89) + (72 \times 0.40) = 296$ kg $= 0.296$ tonne.

Cost allowables:

Labour:	78 NU/0.296 tonne = 263 NU/tonne
Transport:	2 NU/0.296 tonne = 7 NU/tonne

Time allowable:

Labour:
78 NU/3 days = 26 NU/day
(8-hour working day)
263 / 26 = <u>10.1 days/tonne</u> =
0.010 days/kg (= 5 minutes/kg)

3. Formwork to foundations

Cost allowables:

Labour:	52 NU/18 m^2 = 2.9 NU/m^2
Transport:	3 NU/18 m^2 = 0.2 NU/m^2

Time allowable:

Labour:
52 NU/2 days = 26 NU/day
2.9/26 = <u>0.11 days/m^2</u>

5. Steel to columns

12 mm weighs 0.89 kg/m and 8 mm weighs 0.40 kg/m.

That gives us: $(231 \times 0.89) + (76 \times 0.40) = 236$ kg $= 0.236$ tonne

Cost allowables:

Labour:	104 NU/0.236 tonne = 441 NU/tonne
Transport:	2 NU/0.236 tonne = 8 NU/tonne

Time allowable:

Labour:
$$104 \text{ NU}/4 \text{ days} = 26 \text{ NU/day}$$
$$441/26 = \underline{17.0 \text{ days/tonne}} =$$
$$0.017 \text{ days/kg } (= 8 \text{ minutes/kg})$$

6. Formwork to columns

Cost allowables:

Labour: $104 \text{ NU}/49 \text{ m}^2 = 2.1 \text{ NU/m}^2$

Transport: $5 \text{ NU}/49 \text{ m}^2 = 0.1 \text{ NU/m}^2$

Time allowable:

Labour:
$$104 \text{ NU}/4 \text{ days} = 26 \text{ NU/day}$$
$$2.1/26 = \underline{0.08 \text{ days/m}^2}$$

7. Concrete to columns

Cost allowables:

Labour: $112 \text{ NU}/3.7 \text{ m}^3 = 30.3 \text{ NU/m}^3$

Plant: $32 \text{ NU}/3.7 \text{ m}^3 = 8.6 \text{ NU/m}^3$

Transport: $18 \text{ NU}/3.7 \text{ m}^3 = 4.9 \text{ NU/m}^3$

Time allowable:

Labour:
$$112 \text{ NU}/2 \text{ days} = 56 \text{ NU/day}$$
$$30.3 / 56 = \underline{0.54 \text{ days/m}^2}$$

Always remember to make sure that your plant can keep pace with your labour. *In this case* the same as calculations in handbook 2: 0.10 days/m². (Look again at handbook 2, Chapter 2, step 4, for an example.)

8. Concrete block walls up to floor

Cost allowables:

Labour: $93 \text{ NU}/32 \text{ m}^2 = 2.9 \text{ NU/m}^2$

Transport: $30 \text{ NU} / 32 \text{ m}^2 = 0.9 \text{ NU/m}^2$

Time allowable:

Labour:
$$93 \text{ NU}/3 \text{ days} = 31 \text{ NU/day}$$
$$2.9/31 = \underline{0.09 \text{ days/m}^2}$$

If transport is done in advance, it is not a limiting factor.

10. Hardcore fill

Cost allowables:

Labour:	84 NU/17 m^3 = 4.9 NU/m^3
Plant:	24 NU/17 m^3 = 1.4 NU/m^3
Transport:	10 NU/17 m^3 = 0.6 NU/m^3

Time allowable:

Labour: 84 NU/3 days = 28 NU/day
4.9/28 = <u>0.18 days/m^3</u>

Always remember to make sure that your plant can keep pace with your labour. In this case the roller is probably not a limiting factor.

11. Mesh to floor

8 mm bars weighs 0.40 kg/m
That gives us: (325 × 0.40) = 130 kg = 0.130 tonne

Cost allowables:

Labour:	52 NU/0.130 tonne = 400 NU/tonne
Transport:	1 NU/0.130 tonne = 8 NU/tonne

Time allowable:

Labour: 52 NU/2 days = 26 NU/day
400/26 = <u>15.4 days/tonne</u> = 0.015 days/kg

12. Concrete to floor

Cost allowables:

Labour:	168 NU/6.8 m^3 = 24.7 NU/m^3
Plant:	48 NU/6.8 m^3 = 7.1 NU/m^3
Transport:	31 NU/6.8 m^3 = 4.6 NU/m^3

Time allowable:

Labour: 168 NU/3 days = 56 NU/day
24.7/56 = <u>0.44 days/m^2</u>

Always remember to make sure that your plant can keep pace with your labour. In this case the same as calculations in handbook 2: 0.10 days/m^2.

13. Concrete block walls above floor

Cost allowables:

Labour:	93 NU/34 m^2 = 2.7 NU/m^2
Transport:	33 NU/34 m^2 = 1.0 NU/m^2

Time allowable:

Labour:	93 NU/3 days = 31 NU/day
	2.7/31 = <u>0.09 days/m^2</u>

If transport is done in advance, it is not a limiting factor.

17. Steel to ringbeam

12 mm weighs 0.89 kg/m and 8 mm weighs 0.40 kg/m.
That gives us: (144 × 0.89) + (54 × 0.40) = 150 kg = 0.150 tonne

Cost allowables:

Labour:	78 NU/0.150 tonne = 520 NU/tonne
Transport:	2 NU/0.150 tonne = 13 NU/tonne

Time allowable:

Labour:	78 NU/3 days = 26 NU/day
	520/26 = <u>20 days/tonne</u> =
	0.020 days/kg (= 10 minutes/kg)

18. Concrete to ringbeam

Cost allowables:

Labour:	112 NU/2.6 m^3 = 43.1 NU/m^3
Plant:	32 NU/2.6 m^3 = 12.3 NU/m^3
Transport:	12 NU/2.6 m^3 = 4.6 NU/m^3

Time allowable:

Labour:
$$112 \text{ NU}/2 \text{ days} = 56 \text{ NU/day}$$
$$43.1/56 = \underline{0.77 \text{ days/m}^2}$$

Always remember to make sure that your plant can keep pace with your labour. In this case the same as calculations in handbook 2: 0.10 days/m².

Exercise 2   BLOCKMAKER'S ALLOWABLES

A. What are the labour, plant and transport cost allowables per 100 blocks?

Given:	Cost for 10 labourers to make 1,000 blocks	20 NU
Calculated:	Cost for 10 labourers to make 100 blocks	2 NU
	Labour allowable per 100 blocks = 2 NU	
Given:	Cost for plant (mixer) to make 1,000 blocks	20 NU
Calculated:	Plant allowable per 100 blocks = 2 NU	
Given:	Cost of transporting 1,000 blocks	40 NU
Calculated:	Transport allowable per 100 blocks = 4 NU	

B. What will be the final cost to the client per 100 blocks delivered to site?

Labour cost per 100 blocks	2 NU
Plant cost per 100 blocks	2 NU
Transport cost per 100 blocks	4 NU
Material cost per 100 blocs: 60/10 = 6	6 NU
Total cost to make 100 blocks	14 NU
Add 25 per cent profit (0.25 × 14 = 3.5)	3.5 NU
Final cost to the client per 100 blocks (excluding indirect costs)	17.5 NU

Answers to business practice - 3

Exercise 1   CONCRETE FLOOR SLAB

BAR CHART

Item	Week number													
	01	02	03	04	05	06	07	08	09	10	11	12	13	14
1. Access road	══	══	══											
2. Fence site		══	══											
3. Strip topsoil				══										
4. Spread hardcore					══	══								
5. Seal hardcore						══	══							
6. Fix floor mesh							══	══	══					
7. Pour slab and cure								══	══	══	══	══	══	
8. Clear site														══

Answers to business practice - 4

Exercise 1   CAN YOU DELIVER?

It seems impossible to complete this task within eight weeks with only the four carpenters you have available. You should <u>not</u> bid for this job since delivery within eight weeks was made a condition. If you take on this contract you will certainly have to pay damages to the client.

The bar chart below shows a tight but possible time schedule to complete the work within eight weeks. It would however, require up to three times as many carpenters as you have available. It seems impossible to meet the time target under the conditions given, no matter how you plan. See also the comments on individual items which are given after the labour schedules below.

BAR CHART, MANUFACTURING OF FRAMES

Item	Week number							
	01	02	03	04	05	06	07	08
1. Collect materials	═══	═══	═					
2. Cut to size		═	═══					
3. Plane timber		═	═══	═				
4. Moulding and jointing			═	═══	═			
5. Fix frames				═	═══	═		
6. Varnish					═	═══		
7. Deliver to site							═	═══

SEMI-WEEKLY LABOUR SCHEDULE, CARPENTERS

Item	Week number							
	01	02	03	04	05	06	07	08
1. Collect materials								
2. Cut to size		2	2 2					
3. Plane timber		2	2 2	2				
4. Moulding and jointing			4 4	4 4	4 4			
5. Fix frames				4 4	4 4	4		
6. Varnish					4 4	4 4		
7. Deliver to site								
Totals		4	8 8	10 8	12 12	8 4		

SEMI-WEEKLY LABOUR SCHEDULE, GENERAL LABOURERS

Item	Week number 01		02		03		04		05		06		07		08	
1. Collect materials	4	4	4	4	4											
2. Cut to size				4	4	4										
3. Plane timber				4	4	4	4									
4. Moulding and jointing					2	2	2	2	2	2						
5. Fix frames							2	2	2	2	2					
6. Varnish									2	2	2	2				
7. Deliver to site													4	4	4	4
Totals	4	4	4	12	14	10	8	4	6	6	4	2	4	4	4	4

Comments on individual items:

1. Collect materials

Because of the long drive (one day in each direction) this activity will take 2.5 weeks to complete. Although more labourers are available, you cannot really have more than six workers loading and unloading. Using six labourers would only reduce the time for each trip by three hours (2.6 days instead of 3 days). To reduce the time needed for collecting materials there are only two options; either hire an additional truck or try to find a sawmill closer to your workshop.

2. Cut to size

You have two circular saws, therefore you need two carpenters. Although this activity only takes 1.5 weeks to complete, it cannot be finished earlier. You need about half a week after the material arrives on site. It is difficult to speed up this activity without investing in a new circular saw. That cannot normally be justified by a single project.

3. Plane timber

You have two planers, therefore you need two carpenters. This activity can start at the same time as item 2. It is difficult to speed up this activity as only two planers are available.

4. Moulding and jointing

Three weeks is the shortest possible time for this if you only have four carpenters available. No other carpentry work can be done at the same time.

116

5. Fix frames
Two-and-a-half weeks is the shortest possible time to complete this task with four carpenters.

6. Varnish
This takes two weeks to complete with four carpenters.
General comment: items 4-6 can be completed more quickly only if additional carpenters are hired. With careful planning you could probably manage with eight to ten carpenters.

7. Deliver to site
The varnished frames need to dry for approximately two weeks before delivery i.e. this activity can start two weeks after item 6 has started. Like item 1 the time needed for this activity can only be significantly reduced if an additional truck is hired, although hiring two additional labourers improves the situation more than for collecting materials.

Answers to business practice - 5

Exercise 1	PLANT AND TRANSPORT
	SCHEDULES

LIST OF QUANTITIES

Item	Description	Unit	Quantity
1	Strip topsoil and cart to storage area	m³	100
2	Excavate ground and cart to dump	m³	250
3	Load hardcore, spread, level and compact	m³	150
4	Load gravel, spread, level and compact	m³	100

Calculations:

Item 1: 50 m × 20 m × 0.1 m = 100 m³

Item 2: 50 m × 20 m × 0.25 m = 250 m³

Item 3: 0.25 m − 0.10 m = 0.15 m; 50 m × 20 m × 0.15 m = 150 m³

Item 4: 50 m × 20 m × 0.10 m = 100 m³

BAR CHART

Item	Day number
	1 2 3 4 5 6 7 8 9 10 11 12 13 14 15 16 17 18 19 20 21 22 23 24 25 26 27 28 29 30 31
1. Strip topsoil and cart	days 1–3
2. Excavate ground and dump	days 4–9
3a. Load hardcore and tip	days 10–12
3b. Spread and level	days 12–15
3c. Compact	days 16–20
4a. Load gravel and tip	days 20–23
4b. Spread and level	days 23–26
4c. Compact	days 26–31

Calculations to prepare bar chart as well as plant and transport schedule:

1   Strip topsoil and cart to storage area

1 f/e loader working with 2/6 m³ tipper trucks

100 m³/6 m³ = 17 loads

Each load takes 1 hour. 17 h/2 trucks = 8.5 h. Front-end loader loads one at a time i.e. more than 17 hours. We also have to allow some extra time for delays. Result: 3 days

2   Excavate ground and cart to dump

1 f/e loader working with 2/6 m³ tipper trucks

250 m³/6 m³ = 42 loads

42 loads take 84 hours to complete. 84 h/2 trucks = 42 h = 5.3 days. Allowance for delays gives us 6 days.

3   Load hardcore, spread, level and compact

1 f/e loader working with 4/6 m³ tipper trucks

1 grader and 1 roller.

150 m³/6 m³ = 25 loads

25 loads take 75 hours to complete. 75 h/4 trucks = 19 h = 2.4 days. Allowance for delays gives us 3 days to complete activity 3.

Grader for 4 days and roller for 5 days.

4   Load gravel, spread, level and compact

1 f/e loader working with 4/6 m³ tipper trucks

1 grader and 1 roller.

100 m³/6 m³ = 17 loads

17 loads take 68 hours to complete. 68 h/4 trucks = 17 h = 2.1 days. Allowance for delays gives us 3 days to complete activity 4.

Grader for 4 days and roller for 5 days.

PLANT AND TRANSPORT SCHEDULE

Item	Day number
	1 2 3 4 5 6 7 8 9 10 11 12 13 14 15 16 17 18 19 20 21 22 23 24 25 26 27 28 29 30
1. Strip top-soil and cart	Days 1–2 — f/e loader, 2 / 6 m³ tippers
2. Excavate ground and dump	Days 3–8 — f/e loader, 2 / 6 m³ tippers
3a. Load hard-core and tip	Days 9–11 — f/e loader, 4 / 6 m³ tippers
3b. Spread and level	Days 12–18 — grader
3c. Compact	Days 15–26 — roller

120

4a. Load gravel and tip																									f/e loader 4 / 6 m³ tippers					
4b. Spread and level																		grader												
4c. Compact																							roller							
Front-end loader	1	1	1	1	1	1	1	1	1	1	1									1	1	1								
6 m³ tipper trucks	2	2	2	2	2	2	2	2	4	4	4									4	4	4								
Grader											1	1	1	1								1	1	1	1					
Roller															1	1	1	1	1							1	1	1	1	1

Answers to business practice - 6

Exercise 1 COMPLETE THE MATERIALS SCHEDULE

MATERIALS SCHEDULE

							Details of supplier					
Information obtained from calculations of quantities				Date that materials are needed on site (from bar chart)	Time needed between order and delivery (information at planning stage)	Latest date that order must be placed	Order no.	Name	Address	Phone	Contact	Remarks
Item	Description	Unit	Quantity									
27.	Ceiling boards	m^2	126	Week 15 Nov. 7th	2 weeks	Oct. 17th	205	Best Company	Border Road 8	3249	Steve Neale	Allows 2 weeks credit
28.	Window panels	No	12	Week 16 Nov. 14th	1 week	Oct. 31st	211	G Work-shop Ltd.	Long Road 32	1145	Mr. Stone	Cash on delivery
29.	Door panels	No	3	Week 16 Nov. 14th	2 weeks	Oct. 24th	212	Frame Works Ltd.	Panel Road 21	2988	Mr. Knob	Cash with order
30.	Terrazzo	m^2	132	Week 17 Nov. 21st	1 week	Nov. 7th	220	Floor Special Ltd.	Fifth Street 112	8834	Dick	Cash on delivery
32.	Paint	m^2	270	Week 20 Dec 12th	1 week	Nov. 28th	250	Color Company	Drum Street	6487	Mr. Roller	Allows 3 weeks credit

Did you remember to give yourself an extra week to check delivered goods and replace if necessary as recommended in the handbook?

Exercise 2   USING THE MATERIALS SCHEDULE

A. Materials schedule

MATERIALS SCHEDULE

Information obtained from calculations of quantities				Date that materials are needed on site (from bar chart)	Time needed between order and delivery (information at planning stage)	Latest date that order must be placed	Details of supplier					
Item	Description	Unit	Quantity				Order no.	Name	Address	Phone	Contact	Remarks
4.	Door frames	No	10	Week 7	8 weeks	1 week before Week 1	1	Johns' Joinery	Diane Road	25354	John	Delivery 2 weeks late
6.	Window frames	No	40	Week 12	8 weeks	Week 4	2	=	=	=	=	Delivery 1 week late
9.	Roof trusses	No	35	Week 19	8 weeks	Week 11	3	=	=	=	=	Delivery on time
13.	Bedside units	No	40	Week 33	8 weeks	Week 25	4	=	=	=	=	Delivery on time
16.	Doors	No	10	Week 37	8 weeks	Week 29	5	=	=	=	=	Delivery on time
18.	Partition screens	No	40	Week 39	8 weeks	Week 31	6	=	=	=	=	Delivery on time

B. You will *not* be able to keep up with the main contractor's programme.

C. Why is it impossible to deliver on schedule?
   See our comments on the individual items on the next page.

Comments on individual items:

4   Door frames

The site agent did not give you the bar chart until Week 2, but the door frames must be fitted in Week 8. This only allows six weeks for ordering and making the door frames but the workshop requires eight weeks between order and delivery. The main contractor's programme will be delayed by two weeks, as delivery can only be made in Week 10.

6   Window frames

The order can be placed before or during Week 4 but the fabrication of the window frames will not start until Week 11, and the 40 frames will take three weeks to make. Delivery can therefore be made no sooner than Week 13. This delays the main contractor's programme by one week but since item 4 already delayed the programme by two weeks the second delay might not make matters worse.

9   Roof trusses

The order can be placed in time. The workshop can start fabricating the roof trusses during Week 14 and they take four weeks to complete i.e. the 35 trusses can be on site in Week 17, which is two weeks before they are needed.

13, 16   Bedside units, doors and partition screens
and 18
These present another kind of problem. The orders can be placed well in advance but you must remember that the main contractor will not allow you to store your materials for more than two weeks at the site. When ordering you will have to stipulate "Delivery to site no earlier than week x and no later than week y". Here is a little table indicating the earliest and latest possible delivery dates

Item	Earliest delivery	Latest delivery
13. Bedside units	Week 31	Week 33
16. Doors	Week 35	Week 37
18. Partition screens	Week 37	Week 39

for these three items.

There is enough time between the delivery dates for the workshop to deliver in time. And if they do not want to store completed items at the workshop they can manufacture each item and transport it to the site immediately.

Remember: Your contract with the workshop runs over a long period of time (about 35 weeks). Make sure they hold their prices during the entire contract, especially since you ask them not to deliver some items before a certain date.

Answers to business practice - 7

Exercise 1   MARKING UP THE BAR CHART

See the following pages:

BAR CHART - CONSTRUCTION PHASE

Section A

Item	Week number																			
	01	02	03	04	05	06	07	08	09	10	11	12	13	14	15	16	17	18	19	20
1. Excavate foundations																				
2. Fix steel foundations																				
3. Pour concrete to foundations																				
4. Fix steel to columns																				
5. Fix formwork to columns																				
6. Pour concrete to columns																				
7. Fix steel to ringbeam																				

8. Fix formwork to ringbeam	9. Pour concrete to ringbeam	10. Fabricate and fix roof trusses	11. Tile roof	12. Fit infill panels	13. Fix ceiling	14. Fit and glaze windows	15. Paint	16. Clear site

Section B

Item	Week number																			
	01	02	03	04	05	06	07	08	09	10	11	12	13	14	15	16	17	18	19	20
1. Excavate foundations																				
2. Fix steel foundations																				
3. Pour concrete to foundations																				
4. Fix steel to columns																				
5. Fix formwork to columns																				
6. Pour concrete to columns																				
7. Fix steel to ringbeam																				

8. Fix formwork to ringbeam

9. Pour concrete to ringbeam

10. Fabricate and fix roof trusses

11. Tile roof

12. Fit infill panels

13. Fix ceiling

14. Fit and glaze windows

15. Paint

16. Clear site

Section C

Item	Week number																			
	01	02	03	04	05	06	07	08	09	10	11	12	13	14	15	16	17	18	19	20
1. Excavate foundations																				
2. Fix steel foundations																				
3. Pour concrete to foundations																				
4. Fix steel to columns																				
5. Fix form-work to columns																				
6. Pour concrete to columns																				
7. Fix steel to ringbeam																				

8. Fix formwork to ringbeam	9. Pour concrete to ringbeam	10. Fabricate and fix roof trusses	11. Tile roof	12. Fit infill panels	13. Fix ceiling	14. Fit and glaze windows	15. Paint	16. Clear site

131

PROGRAMME SITUATION AT THE END OF WEEK 14

BAR CHART - CONSTRUCTION PHASE

Item	Week number																			
	01	02	03	04	05	06	07	08	09	10	11	12	13	14	15	16	17	18	19	20
1. Excavate foundations		■	■																	
2. Fix steel foundations			■	■																
3. Pour concrete to foundations			■	■	■															
4. Fix steel to columns					■															
5. Fix formwork to columns					■	■														
6. Pour concrete to columns						■	■													
7. Fix steel to ringbeam								■	■											

132

8. Fix formwork to ringbeam	
9. Pour concrete to ringbeam	
10. Fabricate and fix roof trusses	
11. Tile roof	
12. Fit infill panels	
13. Fix ceiling	
14. Fit and glaze windows	
15. Paint	
16. Clear site	

These bars mark a possible solution.

Exercise 3   A FEEDER-ROAD CONTRACT

Section A

The marked-up bar chart tells us that the contract is three months behind schedule with only six months left to complete the contract.

Section B

Revised bar chart

BAR CHART - FEEDER ROADS A, B AND C

Item	Month number														
	01	02	03	04	05	06	07	08	09	10	11	12	13	14	15
1. Road A km 0-2	══	══													
2. Road A km 2-4			══	══											
3. Road B km 0-2					══	══									
4. Road B km 2-4									══						
5. Road B km 4-6											══				
6. Road C km 0-2												══			
7. Road C km 2-4														══	
8. Road C km 4-5															══

Section C

In order to complete the contract on schedule the contractor will have to greatly increase output over the next five months. That will mean a substantial increase in labour and probably also renting some additional equipment. During the last month the contractor can either stick to the revised schedule with increased output and complete the contract a little early or plan to reduce labour and plant resources at the end of Month 14 and complete on schedule.

Answers to business practice - 8

Exercise 1   RECRUITING A SITE AGENT

The calculations should give the following results:

The cost of employing A would be 40,000 NU.

The cost of employing B would be 60,000 NU, but the amount saved would be 1 per cent of 1,000,000 NU, which is 10,000 NU. Hence the cost of employing B would be 60,000 − 10,000 = 50,000 NU.

The cost of employing C would be 80,000 NU, but the amount saved would be 5 per cent of 1,000,000 NU which is 50,000 NU. Hence the cost of employing C would be 80,000 − 50,000 = 30,000 NU.

It appears that C would be the best choice for the job.

Of course, it is not always possible to determine who is the best supervisor just by a simple calculation like this, but this exercise is a reminder that it is not only the supervisor's salary that is important. An experienced supervisor can often save you a lot of money, if given a good working environment.

Exercise 2   MONDAY'S PROBLEMS

This is the procedure we suggest that you follow:

First, arrange the problems in order, putting the most urgent first, e.g.

C _____

A _____

D _____

E _____

B _____

Then note the solutions.

Problem C Contact the block manufacturer immediately and delay further deliveries.

Problem A Get an independent test done on more cubes (take cores if necessary). Arrange for other tests, e.g. Schmidt hammer; tests on aggregate and water purity.
Put the masons to work building blockwork pillars or walls for the Minister's temporary shelter, since this is additional work already sanctioned by the consultant, so it can be claimed. Mix the mortar by hand, and use the labour to lay a lean-mix temporary concrete floor, also mixed by hand.

Problem D Use all labour, plant and available materials to make the site ready for the visit. Remember to plan this kind of temporary job carefully. Draw up a short-term bar chart and present it to the consultant without delay. Show that you intend to make a very favourable impression on the Minister, which will be advantageous to the consultant's reputation.

Problem E In return for your fullest cooperation concerning the Minister's visit you can now reasonably expect pressure to be put on the chief accountant to release your payment.

Problem B Explain your mixer problems to the consultant. Lack of money to pay in advance for repairs could delay site progress, so this becomes another lever to press for release of certificate payment. Meanwhile, try to find the money somewhere to pay for the short-term hire of a replacement mixer.

Answers to business practice - 9

Exercise I   A BAD SITE LAYOUT?

Criticisms of existing layout for the construction of a radio transmitter station:

1. In general, the working area is too spread out, making control more difficult and increasing non-productive travelling time.

2. Site latrines and canteen are too far away, causing loss of time due to unnecessary travelling. No apparent supply of drinking water on site.

3. No security fencing is shown. Probably necessary.

4. Temporary access road should follow line of proposed station access road to avoid duplication of work.

5. Water supply is a problem. Provide more storage space. Can the construction of a borehole be advanced?

6. Surplus excavation should have been led directly to the erosion nullah gully to avoid double handling.

7. Pylon girders have been stacked over foundation bases, necessitating double handling.

8. Stone mason's yard interferes with movement and handling of technical equipment from the sealed containers.

9. Site office badly situated. As the building area rises, the view of the site will be completely blocked.

10. Cement store too far from the mixer.

11. Concrete aggregates tipped haphazardly, causing waste and impurities. Access by truck is also difficult.

12. The hoist is on the wrong side of the building, too far from work areas.

13. Mortar mixing and blockmaking area too far from the building.

14. Temporary buildings and storage areas sited over line of sewer. The sewer should be constructed early to free the ground.

15. Steel laid haphazardly on ground and not stacked neatly. Bending and fabrication benches wrongly placed.

16. Timber storage area appears disorganized.

17. Sanitary fittings, pipes and frames stacked too near access road for safety.

18. There should be a separate cement store.

19. A shaded rest area is most desirable.

20. A workshop should be combined with the timber and steel storage areas.

You should have noted at least 12 - 15 of the points mentioned above.

Exercise 2   YOUR TURN

The figure on page 139 is an example of a revised site plan incorporating the points covered in exercise 1.

Answers to business practice - 10

Exercise 1   WHAT A SITE!

A. The major problems are:
  1. The excavated material has been stacked too close to the excavation
  2. The barrows have to be wheeled over a very narrow plank, which will cause congestion and delay
  3. The mixer and the bowser are badly located
  4. The aggregate piles overlap, which will mean uncontrolled mixing of sand and stone.

Figure 3. Revised site plan

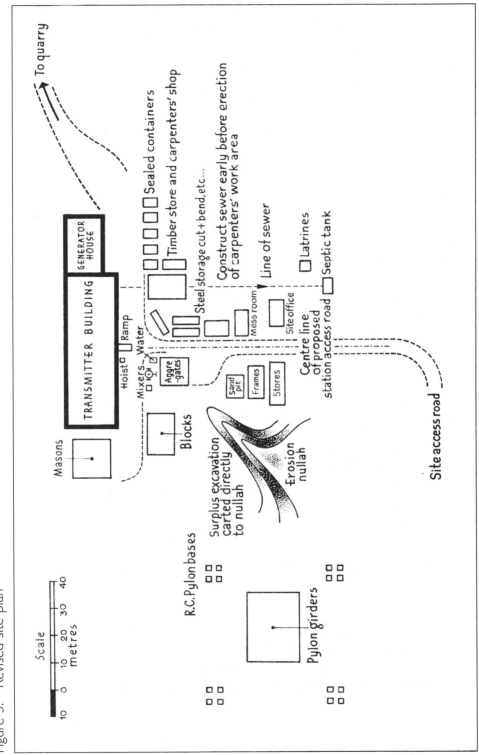

B. The site supervisor should have:
1. Carted away the excavated material before fixing steel in the foundations, then. . .
2. Completed hardcore filling and compacting to the centre of the building so as to give direct barrow access to all parts of the foundations, then. . .
3. Repositioned the bowser and mixer for easier loading, and. . .
4. Separated the sand and the stone with a central barrier.

C. Productivity could still be improved.

Speeding up the mixing, barrowing and placing of the concrete can be achieved by transporting away more of the excavated material. You would then open up better access for barrowing and placing and make it possible for the mixer to be closer to the water bowser.

Exercise 2   CUTTING COSTS

A. The major problems are:
1. Barrowing the sand uphill is exhausting for the labourers, so they will soon tire and their output will drop
2. The front-end loader is underutilized, since the work of stockpiling is relatively quick
3. The labourers are currently loading the truck, so it is standing idle for much of the day.

B. Costs can be cut by using the plant properly to replace the work of the labourers.

C. 1. The front-end loader should travel direct from the quarry face to the truck while the truck is standing, so that wasteful stockpiling is eliminated
2. Sand can be stockpiled by the loader while the truck is away delivering sand, so as to speed up loading when it returns.

Answers to business practice - 11

Exercise 1   WORKING BETTER

❏ The joiner's yard is a disaster area! The best thing to do is to take the week before the contract starts and reorganize the yard. This will mean a change in site layout to improve productivity and workflow. See figure 7 below.

Figure 7.   Change in site layout at joiner's yard

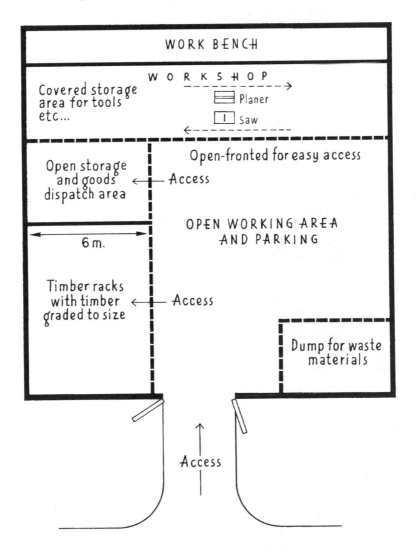

❏ Our main suggestions for reorganization are:
- – Timber should be sized and graded in the racks
- – Labourers bring the timber as the carpenters need it
- – Deliveries should be planned ahead of time
- – The joiner is the company's biggest asset so he should spend more time in the workshop and organize his managerial duties more efficiently
- – The workers should be put on a daily or weekly wage and given incentive payments; trussmaking is ideal for piece work
- – Furniture making should be stopped until the roof truss contract is finished, except for urgent orders from regular customers
- – The owner should offer to deliver the trusses to the housing site at a competitive additional price. This will save the building contractor the cost of collection, and will ensure that finished trusses are dispatched promptly or that the replanned storage area is sufficient.

Answers to business practice - 12

Exercise 1   CHOOSE YOUR METHOD!

OPERATION 1.

A. Either taskwork or piecework

B. It is easy to control when using a large gang on this type of work

C. Through the foreman who will then explain the deal and the task to the workforce.

OPERATION 2.

A. Daily wage

B. If the masons and carpenters were given one of the other methods of payment it would not be fair to them because they will be continually interrupted so that they cannot get on with the job in an organized fashion

C. Supervision by trades foremen, timesheets by wages clerk.

OPERATION 3.

A. Bonus scheme

B. Because strict quality control can be carried out if a bonus is given for finishing within three weeks only if the work is done to a very high standard. The deal would be:

Completed in three weeks, very high standard – very good bonus

Completed one day over time, very high standard – good bonus

Completed two days over time, very high standard – small bonus

Completed three days over time, very high standard – no bonus

Completed in three weeks, below standard – no bonus

C. Supervision by site manager, with strict emphasis on quality control and tough discipline to achieve it.

OPERATION 4.

A. Daily wage

B. Since it is the first time you have been faced with this sort of work you do not know enough to base a target on

C. Supervision by site manager, taking notes and timing individual activities so that next time you can calculate a bonus target that can be achieved and still make money for you.

Answers to business practice - 13

Exercise 1   YOU ARE A SAFETY INSPECTOR!

ACCIDENT REPORT - CASE 1: THE CIRCULAR SAW	
Injury	Very severe cut to left arm
Accident	When the plug on the saw was connected to the extension lead, the machine started and the saw blade acted as a wheel so that it fell off the panels
Cause	1. Socket switch left in "on" position 2. Worker unfamiliar with portable circular saw 3. Saw placed on top of panels 4. Interference with switch of portable tool 5. Defective guard
Responsibility	Supervisor 1. Imprecise instructions 2. Inadequate training of carpenter 3. Allowed earlier misuse of tool 4. Failed to ensure effective periodic inspection of portable electric tools Carpenter 1. Did not inform supervisor of his lack of experience 2. Did not check that the socket switch was in the "off" position 3. Did not inspect portable saw before use 4. Placed saw in dangerous position on top of panels

ACCIDENT REPORT - CASE 2: THE LABOURER AND THE LADDER	
Injury	Fracture of right wrist
Accident	Ladder slipped on metal chequer plate floor as labourer was descending
Cause	1. Ladder at unsafe angle. 2. Ladder neither wedged nor held 3. Ladder was too long for the task
Responsibility	<u>Manager</u> 1. Should have kept his temper and pointed out defects more reasonably <u>Foreman</u> 1. Should have kept his temper and given proper instructions to labourer 2. Allowed dirt to accumulate 3. Allowed top of partition to be used to store old cartons 4. Ladder was not suitable for use in all parts of the department <u>Labourer</u> 1. Used unsuitable ladder 2. Set ladder at unsafe angle

Answers to business practice - 14

Exercise 1   QUALITY CONTROL

A. Figure 9   Straight alignment and accurate width of strip
footings

Answer: Profiles and string lines

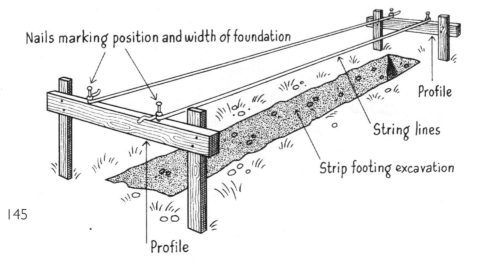

Nails marking position and width of foundation

Profile

String lines

Strip footing excavation

Profile

B. Figure 10.   Accurate levels of an excavation

Answer: Boning rods and sight rails

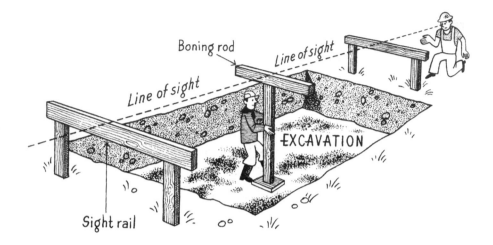

C. Figure 11.   Laying of drainage pipes to correct fall

Answer: String line over tops of collars

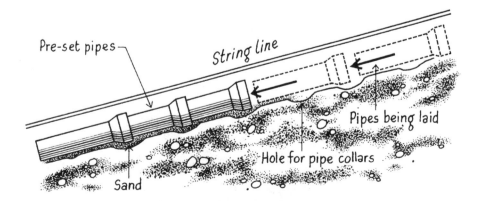

D. Figure 12. Alignment of pipes after laying and before backfill

Answer: Look through the pipes to check that you see a perfect circle of light

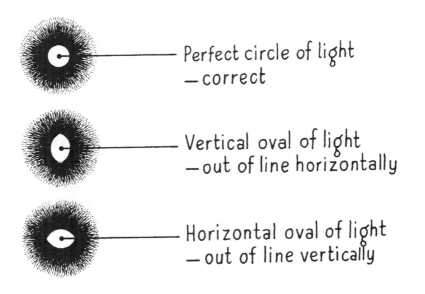

——— Perfect circle of light
— correct

——— Vertical oval of light
— out of line horizontally

——— Horizontal oval of light
— out of line vertically

E. Figure 13. Correct standard width of joints in bathroom tiles

Answer: Use tile spacers

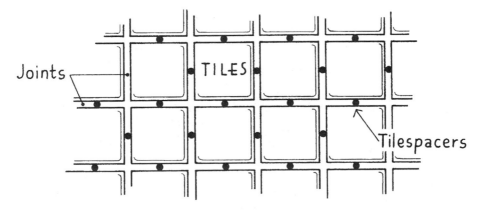

Joints

TILES

Tilespacers

Exercise 2   THE ROOF COLLAPSES

Who is to blame, and why?

The supplier	for supplying a possibly faulty product
The builder	for not checking and testing the lintels before delivery
	for not sending the broken one and the other nine back for testing or,
	for not bringing the supplier to the site to examine them
	for not demanding a written condemnation or clearance from the clerk of works
	for building them into the house
The clerk of works	for not doing his administrative work properly. The lintels should either have been condemned (in writing) or accepted (in writing)

The ultimate blame must be taken by the builder, who has been negligent in his own duties of quality control. Although some of the blame goes to both the supplier and the clerk of works, the builder is finally and solely responsible for the standard of materials and workmanship that go into the job. Unless the client interfered with the lintels after the building was completed, the builder must pay for all the repairs.